YOU'RE HIRED! RESUME TACTICS

JOB SEARCH STRATEGIES THAT WORK

RAE A. STONEHOUSE

Live For Excellence Productions

Rae A. Stonehouse   472 Belrose Drive
Author & Publishing Consultant   Kelowna, B.C.
publisher@liveforexcellence.com   liveforexcellence.com

~

E-book - ISBN: 978-1-9994754-4-4
Print - ISBN: 978-1-9994754-7-5

Live For Excellence Productions
1221 Velrose Drive
Kelowna, B.C., Canada
V1X6R7
https://liveforexcellence.com

CONNECT WITH US

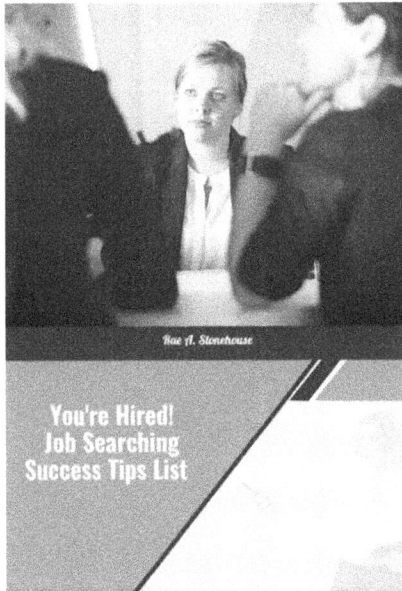

Subscribe to our **You're Hired! Job Search Strategies That Work Newsletter** to receive job searching sage advice from Rae A. Stonehouse and receive **You're Hired! Job Searching Success Tips List**, a free e-book providing you with 55 tips to landing your next job.

http://eepurl.com/ghp73f

Visit us on the web at http://yourehirednow.com.

Check out our **Jobs Now Blog** @ http//yourehirednow.com for job searching advice to frequently asked questions.

For even more job searching tips & techniques, join us on **Facebook** https://www.facebook.com/jobstrategiesthatwork/

Twitter: https://twitter.com/yourehirednow

∼

1. WELCOME!

Hi there! Welcome to **You're Hired! Resume Tactics - Job Search Strategies That Work.**

Make no mistake. Searching for work... is work!

It takes time, effort and a lot of self-motivation to succeed in your search.

While you have your skills and experience in place to be able to apply and land your dream job, or one that leads you to it, searching for a job requires a whole different set of skills.

It is often said 'resumes are your ticket to job searching success.' This book focuses on *resume writing tactics* to maximize your job searching effectiveness and is excerpted and expanded upon, from my book **You're Hired! Job Search Strategies That Work.**

Nobody can make a promise that if you follow their program, you will be guaranteed the results you are looking for and I won't either.

However, I'm confident that if you follow the strategies outlined in this book, your chances of succeeding in landing a job are increased.

From my experience, one of the biggest problems job seekers often face is they feel they are coming from an inferior position and they don't have a lot of personal power. The belief being that the Employer has the superior position and has all the power.

Yes, they have the job and they have the power to give you the job... or not.

What you may not realize is many Hiring Managers are under similar pressures as you, the job seeker. They have the pressure of finding the right candidate for the vacancy they need to fill.

They are accountable to their superiors should the person they hire not work out. It has been said that an inappropriate hire can cost the organization an additional 30 to 50 percent over the job position's annual wage. This would include lost productivity incurred when the new hire is oriented, the cost of advertising for new applicants and the time taken to interview and follow up with applicants.

Hiring managers are under pressure to hire the right candidate.

Your task is to become the *only* choice. The *right* choice!

As I mentioned earlier, we are likely not experts at searching for jobs and landing one. It isn't something we do on a regular basis.

As I researched the content for my book **You're Hired! Job Search Strategies That Work**, I found that the problem is compounded by a lack of hard facts on what are the best-practices for job searching.

I'm reminded of an old parable about a group of blind men that were required to touch an elephant and to describe their observations.

Each one felt a different part, but only one part, such as a tusk or the trunk. When they compared notes, they learned that they were in complete disagreement.

I found the same to be true when researching strategic job searching skills.

Each webpage from my search results on the internet spoke from the perspective of the writer whether they were a resume writer, an Employer Hiring Manager, recruiter, etc.

Much the same as the blind men describing what an elephant looks like, their advice is from their perspective. That makes sense to me. We all create our own reality. My reality is completely different from anyone else's.

The problem is that the job search 'experts' state their observations as hard facts. They believe what they write is true. And then next article you read, will dispute what the first expert had said and they will present their truths.

How can something be both true and false at the same time? You must never do this. You must always do this.

Same advice. Can something be both yes and no?

I don't consider myself an expert at job searching.

What I am very good at though is taking subjects that people struggle with, finding better, easier ways to do things and breaking it down to basic strategies that work.

I create *systems* to solve *problems*.

Years ago, I moved my family across Canada to a city where I didn't know anyone.

I had a brand-new home built for me, but I didn't have a job waiting for me when I got there.

At the time, the new location was very hostile towards people that had moved from the east to the west coast.

I often heard "you Easterners come out here and steal our jobs…"

I found that jobs were limited. I found getting an interview for a position I had applied for was like winning a lottery.

I also found that my new geographical area had what they called a 'Sunshine Tax.'

As a desirable place to live, the cost of living is higher and employers believe that they can get away with paying their employees lower wages. The idea being that you the worker should be grateful to have a job and that the employer can get away with paying you less.

'If you don't want the job, somebody else will!"

I got so tired of hearing about stealing local jobs that I started to change my story when I attended local business networking events.

Instead of saying that I was *unemployed*, I would say that I had *retired* early.

I was 39 years old and the illusion that I had retired early seem to resolve the 'you Easterners' complaint.

However, I used to add "if the right job came along, I would likely consider going back to work."

It was offered somewhat tongue in cheek.

It took me a good six months to land a job. It wasn't as good a job as I had hoped.

It was a compromise until something better came along.

I describe my employment experience at my new location as being like a roller coaster ride.

I went from being unemployed, to employed. I went from not getting enough hours to getting too many.

I went from being employed to being laid off.

I went from being employed to being self-employed.

Self-employment ended when I came back from a vacation to find that my only client had sold their business i.e. a vocational school and the new owners had no idea who I was or had need of my services.

Back to being unemployed.

Then I got a job in another city. It was a 90-mile round trip, daily.

I went from being at the employer's beck and call for three years working as many hours as I could as a casual staff. Then I got fired!

Then I got *unfired* and a new job, same company, a few blocks away.

I went from full time to no time to part time to even more part time. Then less time and even less time.

I had to tell my manager that I couldn't afford to stay and I couldn't afford to go.

We solved the problem by me picking up hours from another worker who wanted to work less.

The downside is that I work a lot of night shifts and it is still a 90 mile, 150-kilometre round trip for work.

I think you can see why I call it a roller coaster ride.

Over the years, I have been invited to numerous job search training programs as a guest speaker, promoting the value of public speaking skills and networking to the job search and interviewing process.

Throughout this book, I will be providing you with what I consider to be best practices for creating and writing your resume.

Some content may disagree with what the so-called experts would say but then again... the next one would likely agree with me.

If you are a sports fan, you will recognize that any sport has a set of rules and varying degrees of competition.

Searching for a job, your job, is a competitive situation.

It could come down to two or more possible candidates, hopefully you, being one of them, having very similar credentials and qualifications.

If there was ever a time that self-promotional skills and self-confidence would come into play, it would be in the job searching and interviewing process.

Being able to effectively promote yourself can make the difference between landing the job and a 'thank you very much, but we won't be hiring you at this time."

Welcome aboard and I hope you enjoy our journey together!

2. RESUMES OVERVIEW

Y ou would think that creating a resumé would be an easy task. Even spelling it looks a little weird.

In Canada, resumé is the sole spelling given by the Canadian Oxford Dictionary; résumé is the only spelling given by the Gage Canadian Dictionary (1997 edition).

In the US & Canada, there are three major spellings of this word: résumé, resumé, and resume. And that comes from Wiktionary.

You will likely see several different spellings throughout this book.

They are all acceptable.

I would expect that if you were searching the internet for advice on how to create a resumé, you would become awfully frustrated. I know that I certainly was.

There is the old-school way of creating one and the so-called new ways to create a resumé.

The problem seems to be that nobody really seems to agree on what the new way is.

Everybody has their own 'pearls of wisdom' that has either worked for them or is based on their personal perspective of the job-searching process.

If you dig deep enough, you will notice patterns on the advice given. Each piece of sage advice to the positive seemingly has someone else who believes the opposite.

Much of the resumé writing advice is given in absolute positives 'you must do this!", 'you must never do this!' or 'that is so out-dated... here is how you do it now!'

'Write for a robot resume reader' or 'don't write for a robot resume reader. That's so 2016!'

What I have tried to do is to create a system to help you create your resumé, yourself.

I've highlighted techniques and tactics gathered from self-proclaimed experts on the internet and have organized them in a manner that should make it easier for you to decide for yourself and create a winning resumé.

So, what is the purpose of a resumé?

If you're fairly new to job searching, you might have been led to believe that a resumé is the document that gets you hired.

That's not precisely how it works.

Your resumé is indeed the document you use to apply for jobs (along with a customized Cover Letter where appropriate).

However, the real function of your resumé is to simply whet the employer's appetite and get them to want to call you for an interview.

It's critical to always bear in mind that your resumé is a tool with one specific purpose: to win an interview.

Some people write a resumé as if the purpose of the document was to land a job. As a result, they end up with a really long and boring piece that makes them look like desperate job hunters.

The *objective* of your resumé is to land an interview and the interview will land you the job (hopefully!).

Your resumé is not a place to brag; nor is it a place to be modest. Its sole purpose is to generate interest in you.

What differentiates you from the competition?

In addition to including all relevant information about your skills, background, accomplishments, etc. you should find ways to include details that could generate curiosity.

If you are new to the job market, perhaps you are just out of school and haven't developed a repertoire of skills yet, you may find yourself looking for what is called an entry-level job.

You may find yourself dropping your resumé off at various businesses with the hope that they may have a vacancy and your resumé might entice them to call you. In this case, your resumé becomes a 'leave behind.'

I'm reminded of a couple local young fellows who didn't quite understand the concept of 'leave behind.'

The two of them were on their way to drop off some resumés at local businesses in the hope of finding some work.

For whatever reason, they decided to do a B&E, that is a break and enter of a home, on the way to pass out their resumés.

Being very polite, when they broke into the house, they took their shoes off at the door, so they wouldn't make a mess.

When they were finished with burglarizing the home, they went on their merry way, back to dropping off their resumés.

There was one big problem though.

In their haste to get away from the house, they had put their shoes on and closed the door, but one fellow inadvertently left his resumé on the floor beside where his shoes had been.

I can feel you wincing.

Yes, this is one leave behind that you never want to do. I'm pretty sure he got an interview, but not quite the one he had hoped for.

Who is going to read your resumé?

It depends on the job you are applying for and where it is located.

For a larger company, there may be a Hiring Manager, whose duty is to review resumés for specific job vacancies.

A smaller organization may have a manager who finds themselves having to fill two or three vacancies a year. Then there are those managers that find themselves hiring for the first time.

You also have Recruiters who are paid on commission for every successful candidate that they place into a job vacancy.

The hiring managers for large companies may use software i.e. robots, to review incoming resumés, sorting them into 'yes' for follow-up by human, or 'no' straight to the waste-paper basket or Trash in cyberspeak.

You supposedly only have *5 to 6 seconds* to impress or catch the eye of a hiring manager that may be tasked with reading several hundred resumes for a single job.

But then again, they may only get a few resumes in each mail delivery.

You need to create a resume that not only catches the attention of whoever receives them, but you want them to dig deeper and contact you for an interview.

Your resume's purpose is to get you called for an interview, not to get you the job.

∾

IN THE NEXT CHAPTER, WE WILL LOOK AT HOW GRAMMAR, SPELLING AND formatting can help you get invited for a job interview... or not!

"THE OBSTACLES YOU FACE ARE... MENTAL BARRIERS WHICH CAN BE broken by adopting a more positive approach."— Clarence Blasier

"OBSTACLES DON'T MATTER VERY MUCH. PAIN OR OTHER circumstances can be there, but if you want something bad enough, you'll find a way to get it." — Max Steingart

"WHAT WOULD YOU DO IF YOU KNEW YOU COULDN'T FAIL?" — ROBERT Schuller

3. GRAMMAR AND SPELLING/FORMATTING

I t goes without saying... avoid spelling or grammatical errors but I'll say it anyway "avoid spelling or grammatical errors!"

Yet, it may well be one of the biggest reasons that job seekers are not called for an interview. There are some recruiters who will discount your resumé the second they see a spelling or grammatical error.

Your eyes often see what you meant to type instead of what's really there.

Although it can be painful, make sure you don't just read over your resume several times, but also that you have a friend take a peak, too.

You would be well off to locate a friend that has good grammatical skills, or you could pay someone to review your resume. It's easy to miss even big, embarrassing mistakes when you've been looking at your resumé for too long.

An objective reader can make a big difference in helping you catch spelling and grammar problems as well as many of the other mistakes identified in this section.

It is important to proofread carefully if you are applying for jobs that require writing skills and/or attention to detail. For a potential future boss, your resume is your first work sample and should reflect your ability to write, edit, and proofread if hired.

Let's look at some specifics:

Watch Your Tenses

Improper tense is another common error that can hurt you in the eyes of hiring managers.

If you are still actively working in the role you are describing, use the present tense and use words such as *manage, deliver, organize.*

If you are describing roles you have had in the **past**, use past-tense verbs. Some examples are 'managed, delivered, organized.'

Avoid First Person Pronouns

As a general practice, don't use words like "I" or "me" or "my."

So, instead of saying "*I* hit and exceeded company sales quotas 100% of the time" say "Hit and exceeded sales quotas 100% of the time."

Employers look at your profiles to see if they can find out more about your qualifications, to see if you are creative, and to see if you'll be a good fit with their team.

They'll also be watching for red flags such as poor grammar and spelling, anti-social behaviour, or anger issues.

CONSISTENCY

Your resumé must be error-free.

That means no spelling errors, no typos. No grammar, syntax, or punctuation errors.

In addition, there should be no errors of fact.

Any recruiter or hiring manager will tell you that such errors make it easy to weed out a resumé immediately.

You should list your information in a consistent way.

Let's take a closer look at formatting.

You want your resumé to stand out, but there is such a thing as standing out in a bad way. You may think it's creative to use 6 different fonts and colors, but that kind of creativity tends to just look clumsy.

Avoid too many font types and steer clear of font sizes that are too big or too small. Big fonts make you look like you are SHOUTING (and can also indicate that you don't have enough good content to fill a resumé with normal-size text).

Small fonts may help you keep your resumé to one page, but it's not worth it if the reader needs to squint.

You should also avoid long paragraphs and long blocks of text.

Most people scan resumés very quickly and often skip long paragraphs and miss key information.

Use white space and bullets to make your resumé format easy on the eye. Use of bullets can also ensure better reader comprehension when visually scanned.

You should leave comfortable margins on the page and make sure that everything is aligned. Look neat. Look smart.

Also, keep in mind that there's a good chance your resumé will be scanned electronically as more and more companies use special software to index resumes.

If you're using wacky fonts, the software may not pick up important keywords in your resumé.

Save and send your resumé as a PDF, rather than a Word document, as it freezes it as an image so you can be sure hiring managers see the same formatting as you.

If you send it any other way, there's a chance that the styling, format, font and so on, could look different on their computer than yours.

Labeling your resumé file correctly is important.

Too many people save this important document with random or generic file names like sgks123.pdf or resume.pdf.

Remember that recruiters will see the name of the file that you send them and also remember that they get tons of resumés every day. Make it super clear whose resumé they should click on by saving it under a logical name like FirstName_LastName_Resume.pdf.

I also include the date I created the file as part of my file name. Doing so can be helpful if you have multiple versions saved of your resumé.

Even more important than naming the file in a logical manner is laying out your resume in an organized manner.

How you lay it out depends on where you are in your career path and what you're looking to do next.

While a chronological approach is the default format, it's not always the best way to make your case.

I want to reinforce here that you need to be consistent with your formatting.

For example, if you bold the name of the organization in one section, you need to do it everywhere. Yet at the same time, be sparing with your bolding.

Your formatting should emphasize and reinforce the focus you chose, not distract from it.

As an example of consistence, every job identified on your resumé should list information in this order:

Title

Name of Employer

City and State or Province, depending on where you live and the years you worked there.

Use **boldface**, <u>underlining</u>, and *italics* consistently.

If you decide to **bold** one job title, all titles should be in boldface.

If you <u>underline</u> one section heading, underline them all.

In addition, you should be uniform in your use of capital letters, bullets, dashes, hyphens, etc.

So, if there is a period after one set of job dates, there should be a period after all job dates.

If one degree is in bold, all degrees should be in bold.

Whatever you decide about such things stylistically, be consistent.

It may seem obvious, but spelling and grammar are critical—even if you are in computer programming or sales.

Spell check is not foolproof. Just because it's a word doesn't mean it's the word you want to use.

A grammar error or misspelling can stand out like a sore thumb and tell the employer that you're careless. These mistakes are easily avoidable.

∼

IN THE NEXT CHAPTER, WE LOOK AT HOW TO FEATURE YOUR CONTACT information.

"DON'T SAY, "IF I COULD, I WOULD." SAY, "IF I CAN, I WILL." JIM ROHN

"WE MUST LEARN TO APPLY ALL THAT WE KNOW SO THAT WE CAN attract all that we want." — Jim Rohn

"EVERYTHING COMES TO HIM WHO HUSTLES WHILE HE WAITS." — Thomas Edison

"MAKING A LIVING IS EITHER A STAIRWAY TO A COFFIN... OR A STEPPING stone to greatness... your path awaits you." — Doug Firebaugh

4. CONTACT INFORMATION

I n this chapter, we look at the correct way to use your contact information on your resume.

AFTER ALL, THAT IS THE MAIN PURPOSE OF THE RESUME IN THE FIRST place. You want them to contact you to arrange for an interview. Let's make it easy for them.

. . .

PUT YOUR NAME AT THE BEGINNING OF YOUR RESUMÉ, WITH CONTACT information on separate lines, immediately following your name.

Include mailing address, telephone number with voicemail, professional e-mail address.

Avoid slang or nicknames in your e-mail address.

Buckaroo Bonzo @ Hotmail.com might work for you if you a rodeo star but not so well in the corporate world.

A G-mail e-mail address is considered more professional than a Hotmail or Yahoo one.

Make it easier to contact you by hyperlinking your email address so you're only one click away.

Make sure you have control of and access to all e-mail and phone numbers used. You only need to include one of each (e.g. you can use your cell phone number if you have voicemail).

Your voice mail should have a pleasant and professional welcoming message. It doesn't have to be your voice. It might be better to use your personal cell phone as a contact rather than have a family member answer for you when the big call comes.

Use between two and four lines for contact information.

Make your name a few font sizes larger than other information so that it stands out.

If you've moved or changed phone numbers, make sure that your phone number, address and e-mail information is up to date.

You can include all social media profiles relevant to the application.

LinkedIn is the first on this list, followed by Twitter and the rest.

However, resist the temptation of including all your profiles, because while creative designers may need to include their Instagram profiles, accountants and engineers may not.

If you are going to post your social profiles, you need to ensure that they are professional in nature and up to date.

We'll talk about your social profiles in greater detail later in the program.

~

IN THE NEXT CHAPTER, WE WILL LOOK AT YOUR OBJECTIVE STATEMENT.

5. OBJECTIVE STATEMENT: IN OR OUT?

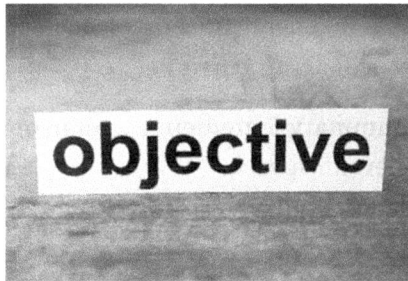

S tarting your resumé off with an **Objective Statement** is one of the many 'new' rules.

Short version... don't do it.

Why not, you might ask?

Traditionally, many resumés have begun with an opening paragraph about what the job seeker is looking for in their next role.

Employers spend little time on their initial scan of resumés and a paragraph about your objectives has none of the things they are looking for.

So, this is a waste of valuable real-estate that can harm your chances.

According to the so-called experts, don't begin your resumé with an objective statement that describes your desires and career goals.

Today's hiring managers aren't concerned with what is it you're looking for—they're focused on finding the right hire. Even the most caring senior executive doesn't care what you are looking for – he only cares about "what's in it for me?"

He or she may care about what you want later when they know you, but for now it's all about them.

This means you need to replace the objective statement with a powerful summary that shows how you will add value to potential employers. The key is to demonstrate to the reader that there is a clear fit between your skills and their needs.

This is where the **Summary Statement** comes in or what some like to call your 'written elevator speech.'

We'll expand upon preparing your Summary Statements shortly.

Resumé Summary Statements

Now that we know *Objective Statements* are out and *Summary Statements* are in... let's take a closer look at them.

Here are the Basics — Your Summary Statement should comprise of a title and a few lines of text.

The text can be in paragraph form and/or use bullets. The Summary Statement should appear directly below your contact information at the top of the resumé and should show the general (or specific) idea of your career goals.

Starting off with...

Your Title: This should communicate your professional identity.

Think of it as a headline that will catch the reader's eye and help them see your fit for the position at hand.

Some examples might include Social Media Brand Strategist, Senior Marketing Executive, Multifaceted Art Director and Global Operations Professional.

We talk about it elsewhere, but the title you use here in your resume's Summary Statement should be consistent with your title on your Linkedin profile.

It also means you must customize your resumé at least slightly for each job opportunity.

Make sure that the Summary Statement is customized based on the job description if you want to catch the hiring manager's eye.

Next, we need to look at the *Format* — The main body of your Summary Statement should be 3-4 lines of text and should NOT be written with first-person pronouns.

If you are tempted to make your Summary Statement longer to squeeze in more details, resist the temptation.

As we have said, most hiring managers spend only seconds reviewing a resumé before they make up their minds to call a candidate or not. We also know when they see large chunks of text, their eyes will skip over it.

Therefore, it is vital to limit the length of a Summary Statement to ensure it gets read.

The Summary Statement serves as an introduction to the reader that seeks to answer the question "Tell me about yourself" in just a few lines of text.

The resume Summary Statement will help your resumé stand out by:

- Catching the reader's attention immediately
- Ensuring a clear understanding of your top selling points at

a glance (important when hiring managers are skimming through dozens of resumés at a time and attention spans are short)

- Putting emphasis on your career highlights and key strengths in an easy-to-scan format
- Briefly communicating your professional objective if relevant (if the objective is not obvious)

EVERY RESUMÉ CAN BENEFIT FROM A SUMMARY STATEMENT. FOR SOME candidates, it can be critical.

Here are some specific groups of job seekers that can benefit from using Summary Statements in their resume.

1. **Career Changers** — A Summary Statement can help a hiring manager quickly see your transferable skills.

Without a Summary Statement, a recruiter might look at your most recent experience, assume you're not a fit because your experience isn't traditional and toss your resumé.

2. **Recent College Grads** — A Summary Statement can help you customize your resumé for different opportunities.

This is especially helpful if your background is somewhat general.

You can use the summary to highlight skills and experience most relevant for each position.

3. **Experienced Professionals with Diverse Backgrounds** — For experienced professionals, a Summary Statement can become the 'executive summary' of your resumé, tailored for each position.

This allows you to pull the most relevant and impressive skills and career accomplishments and feature them at the top of your resumé.

. . .

NEXT, WE ARE GOING TO LOOK AT *HOW* TO WRITE YOUR RESUMÉ Summary Statements.

Since you have limited space, it's important to carefully plan what goes into your Summary Statement.

Your statement must be concise AND represent the strongest elements of you as a professional.

Here are three steps to writing a strong Summary Statement for your resumé:

Step 1: First, think of three or four skills that define you as a professional.

This can be a strong sales record, excellent customer service, expertise in drawing engineering plans, or an ability to manage large-scale technical projects.

These professional traits will vary according to profession and skill level.

Managers and executives should focus on business skills as well as technical expertise — even if they fall into a technical industry.

Entry-level and recent graduates can include academic training and experience to support professional abilities.

Step 2: Next, think of the things you enjoy the most in your work.

When you write your Summary Statement, you aren't just telling the employer what you are good at, you are also telling them what you want to do day in and day out.

Therefore, no matter how well you do something – don't talk about it if you don't want to do it.

Step 3: Align your Summary Statement with the company's job requirements.

Once you identify the skills you want to focus on, do some research and see if they line up with job requirements listed for the positions you are seeking.

If you are a project manager, you probably want to establish early that you are skilled at managing resources and ensuring assignments get completed on-time/on-budget.

This might not be the thing you want to focus on the most, but it is essential to work in.

~

IN THE NEXT CHAPTER, WE LOOK AT SOME EXAMPLES OF 'WRITTEN elevator speeches' or summary/branding statements with titles.

6. WRITTEN ELEVATOR SPEECHES OR SUMMARY/BRANDING STATEMENTS WITH TITLES

Our first example is for a **PROFESSIONAL WRITER.**

A versatile and creative writer fuses a background in journalism and academics with expertise in business writing to deliver quality, customized material spanning news, marketing, web content, curriculum, and career development.

Provides sales support and highly rated client service and excels in meeting deadlines in quick-turnaround settings.

Our second is example is for a **FINANCIAL & OPERATIONS SUPPORT PROFESSIONAL**

Blends academic training in economics and business administration with hands-on experience in sales and operations support to offer employers a track record of delivering on tasks accurately, efficiently, and quickly.

Known for providing best-in-class customer service and communications in a variety of business settings.

. . .

WHAT WE CAN SEE FROM THESE TWO EXAMPLES IS THAT THEY ARE SHORT and to the point.

There should be no confusion or misunderstanding in the mind of the Hiring Manager as to what the applicant is all about.

Here are more helpful Tips on creating your Resumé Summary Statement.

TIP 1. CUSTOMIZE IT FOR YOUR EXPERIENCE LEVEL

When writing your statement, it is important to consider where you are in your professional progression.

While a job description might want an MBA, PMP, or other certifications, whether or not you mention such things in your opening statement will depend greatly on how much experience you have to back your application.

If you are a young job seeker and don't have a history of jobs to refer to it's okay to rely on your academic experience to strengthen your qualifications.

And it is best to call that out from the start.

Here is an example:

This one is for a **BIOLOGY GRADUATE.**

Blends lab management experience with academic training at the University of Victoria to offer solid skills in clinical experiments and research activities.

Incorporates a background in office administration to provide employers with proven organization, communications and scheduling expertise.

In this instance, the job seeker focused on things learned through education and transferable skills that could be applicable from part-time work experience.

On the other hand, if you have strong experience, there is no need to rely on your academic training any longer and it doesn't need to be mentioned.

TIP 2. FOCUS ON YOUR MOST IMPORTANT SELLING POINTS

Some requirements can be covered in the body of the resumé and just aren't important enough to place in that opening paragraph.

One example is proficiency in MS Office.

Even if you are a technical professional, software and hardware skills need their own section on the resumé and don't belong in the opening statement.

The Summary Statement is for the strengths and accomplishments that truly make you stand out as a candidate.

Of course, there are other things you might want to call to the reader's attention early, including language proficiencies, award-winning performance, or being named on one or more patents.

While these qualifications can be contained in the body of a resumé (and should still be placed there), it could be relevant to highlight them early to establish your unique value as an employee.

TIP 3. SKIP THE "I" AND "ME" STUFF

Don't start your opening paragraphs with first person pronouns. An example would be "I did this... then I did such and such."

While you do write the paragraph in present tense, you write it as if you are the understood subject of the resumé. This allows the focus to remain on the employer.

Use of "I, me, my" places the focus on the applicant and the goal of the resumé is to sell the employer on what you can do for THEM.

By telling the reader what you *"do"* and what you are *"known for,"* you get the reader thinking about how you can do those things for them.

This message should be reinforced throughout the resumé as you use achievements and certifications to reinforce your opening paragraph and highlight examples of when you have done the things that your Summary Statement promotes.

$\sim$

IN THE NEXT CHAPTER, WE EXPLORE THE PRACTICE OF SENDING A COVER letter with your resume. Should you, or shouldn't you? We'll see!

7. COVER LETTERS

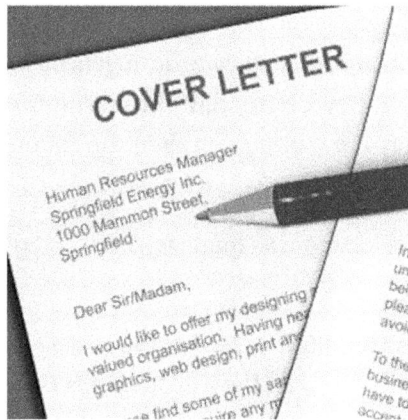

C over letters seem to be another one in the 'are they in or out of fashion' categories.

It likely depends on who you talk to.

There seems to be a trend that many Employers don't seem to adhere to a standardized process for receiving cover letters on their corporate Websites.

Some sites have space to upload or paste in a cover letter; others do not.

Job seekers are less likely to write a 'formal' cover letter when e-mailing their resumés to others.

A simple note such as ("Looking forward to speaking more about [xyz] might suffice. Or...

"My resumé is attached.") is not uncommon.

Whether it is as effective as including a more formalized cover letter, remains to be seen.

It turns out that with **Applicant Tracking Systems (ATS)** what some people call robots, often taking the first pass at screening resumes, the cover letter is often never actually read.

If a resumé contains the right keywords, it gets past the software filters and can be read by a human. If the recruiter sees the skills and experience that they are looking for, then the resumé can be short-listed for a phone call – otherwise it's passed over.

In either case, the decision was made without referring to a cover letter.

One of the most common mistakes people make is to create a standard resumé and send it to all the job openings they can find. Sure, it will save you time, but it will also greatly decrease the chances of landing an interview (so in reality it could even represent a waste of time).

In the **Applicant Tracking Systems** (ATS) era, where cover letters are often not read, this equals sending a generic application with no job or employer-specific customization. Those quickly get tossed.

Tailor your resumé for each employer. The same point applies to your cover letters.

It is important to keep to the employer's submission requirements.

Above all, you won't get noticed if you don't follow all of the specific requirements that have been instructed in the job description.

Often both resumés and cover letters are requested in a certain file format (doc, pdf, docx, rtt).

Sometimes advertisements request applications be sent or addressed in a specific way. Adhere to these, and you'll be one step ahead of any other applicants who didn't bother to tune into this detail!

Whether a cover letter is requested or not, I believe there is value in creating one, even if it just helps you clarify and wrap your head around the specific job you are applying for. You don't necessarily have to send it.

Tell what you know about the employer, its products and services, customers, industry and competition either on your resumé or cover letters; this will show the hiring manager or recruiter you are particularly interested in their job and have done your homework.

This extra work on your part could create instant interview opportunities for you and perhaps help you answer some interview questions when you land the interview.

A Pro Tip about creating cover letters is to use a combination of paragraphs and bulleted lists to convey your information. And don't forget to keep your cover letter on one page, otherwise it may not be read.

$$\sim$$

IN THE NEXT CHAPTER, WE LOOK AT HOW TO LEVERAGE YOUR WORK experience.

8. EXPERIENCE SECTION - SKILLS & ACCOMPLISHMENTS

I n a resume, *experience*, is another way for saying employers are looking for positions you have held in the past.

The *'Old School'* way of completing this section would be to list all your skills to showcase how experienced you were under each job listing.

Here is yet another example of how times have changed.

The purpose of this section is to highlight your top three to five qualifications to a potential employer, from each previous job position.

Your content needs to be crafted so it features you as a solution to the Employer's problem.

If you include this section and you should... use a bullet format and highlight only the skills and/or qualifications relevant to the position you are applying for.

And substantiate with a *brief* explanation of the experience(s) that helped you build that skill or quality.

We will talk about using keywords later in this program.

Career experts recommend that you customize your resumé for *each* job, especially at the beginning of your resumé.

General or generic resumes *do not work* in today's labour market.

For some jobs, you can change a few sentences to focus on certain skills and accomplishments. For others, you may need a *completely new* resumé.

Employers value the skills you have developed, regardless of where you developed them.

This includes skills developed in school, volunteering, extra-curricular activities and in paid employment. Since many employers use past performances to determine whether a candidate will be successful on the job or not; emphasize what you can offer potential employers (or bring to the table) drawing upon your collective experiences, skills, accomplishments, training/education and capabilities.

Validate all relevant successes and contributions made to past employers using numbers, dollars or percentages wherever possible.

Link your experience, skills and abilities to the competency requirements of the job you are applying for using examples of past successes on the job; this will enable the recruiter or hiring manager to visualize you performing the same or a similar role successfully for their organization.

It's easy for people to put any set of skills or abilities on their resumes, but unless you can show those skills in action and the results you got with them, you may not make it to the interview.

Accomplishment statements will demonstrate that you're someone who can get the job done and do it better than other applicants.

Here's another way of looking at it.

When you get to your work experience, don't just list titles and dates. Use a few lines of text to weave a story for hiring managers.

Remember a time in your previous work history when you accomplished something beyond your usual job duties.

Depending on the job and the skills you want to highlight, this 'accomplishment' could be anything between resolving an issue with an upset customer to achieving one million dollars in sales within one year.

Here are some examples:

- When did you change industries?
- Why were you promoted?
- Where do you aim to go next?

The only way to make yourself look unique is to dig into what you did beyond the expected. Just remember to make it reflect one of the skills asked for in the job posting.

Then, use bullet points to back your claims with relevant facts and figures.

STATISTICS ARE AN EASY WAY TO PROVE YOU DID MORE THAN THE JOB description demanded.

. . .

Many professional resumé writers use a technique called **CAR or SAR** statements.

Essentially, you're sharing a challenge/situation/problem, the action you took to address it, and what the result was. Ideally you want to frame the result by sharing how it positively impacted your employer or client.

These are the kinds of statements that make impact and tell a story but also give the reader context. Remember to keep it short; mercilessly edit it down to the least common denominator.

In resumé writing it's also a wise practice to lead with the result/impact to the client or employer because this is usually quantifiable.

Here is a quick example of what I mean by a S.A.R. statement:

Situation/Challenge/Problem: Company operated at a loss of $960,000 in 2014.

Action: Personally vetted by CEO for company turnaround. Cut costs by 30%, revamped hiring practices to reduce turnover, overhauled budget and spending practices.

Result/Impact: Delivered $650,000 profit in 2015.

You can likely use the same format as the example to write your accomplishment statements.

Also note: No bot, nor human, is looking *specifically* for soft skills.

So, delete overused phrases like 'quick learner', 'hard worker' and 'great attitude' and sub in a list of hard skills.

Distinguishable tech and social media knowledge is particularly relevant in today's job market, and no, the Microsoft Office suite doesn't really count, unless the job posting is looking for proficiency in it.

If you're having trouble completing this section, you might have luck by looking to past performance reviews for ideas.

What have your bosses and coworkers said you do better than anyone else?

Or, some might put it as, "What is your superpower?"

Differentiate this section from the *summary* at the top of your resume by focusing on quantifiable evidence. Think dollar signs and percentage points.

As I was writing this last section it occurred to me that the previous advice and perhaps a lot of it applies to someone who is applying for a job in the business sector.

But what about those of us working in the healthcare sector or other service industries? We may not have any access to being able to influence the financial health of the company.

I would think removing financial references and substituting customer satisfaction, how complaints were handled and/or quantifiable results from your specific industry would be a good substitution.

This will take a little work and creativity on your part. Well, probably a lot of work.

~

IN THE NEXT CHAPTER, WE LOOK AT HOW TO HIGHLIGHT YOUR education.

9. EDUCATION

I n this chapter, we are looking at how to showcase your education and a few other miscellaneous items worth mentioning.

List your education in reverse chronological order... degrees or licenses first, followed by certificates and advanced training. Set degrees apart so they are easily seen.

Put in **boldface** whatever will be most impressive.

Include advanced training, but be selective with the information, summarizing the information and including only what will be impressive for the reader.

No degree yet? If you are working on an uncompleted degree, include the degree and afterwards, in parentheses, the expected date of completion: B.S. (expected 20__).

If you didn't finish college, start with a phrase describing the field studied, then the school, then the dates (the fact that there was no degree may be missed).

You might want to use a different heading on your resume rather than Education.

Other headings might be 'Education and Training', 'Education and Licenses', 'Legal Education / Undergraduate Education' (for attorneys).

AWARDS

If the only awards you have received were in school, put these under the Education section.

Mention *what* the award was for if you can or just "for outstanding accomplishment" or "outstanding performance". If you *have* received awards, this section is almost a must.

If you have received commendations or praise from some very senior source, you could call this section, 'Awards and Commendations.' In that case, quote the source.

PROFESSIONAL AFFILIATIONS

Include only those that are current, relevant and impressive. Include leadership roles if appropriate.

This is a good section for communicating your status as a member of a minority targeted for special consideration by employers, or for showing your membership in an association that would enhance your appeal as a prospective employee.

This section can be combined with 'Civic / Community Leadership' as 'Professional and Community Memberships.'

Languages

Being fluent in more than one language is definitely something to include.

Civic / Community Leadership

This is good section to include if the leadership roles or accomplishments you have taken on are related to the job target and can show skills acquired.

For example, a loan officer hoping to become a financial investment counsellor who was Financial Manager of a community organization charged with investing its funds.

Any Board of Directors membership or 'chairmanship' would be good to include.

Be careful with political affiliations, as they could be a plus or minus with an employer or company.

Publications

Include only if published and provide links where you can if you think the work is impressive and relevant. Summarize if there are many.

. . .

Comments from Supervisors, Clients, Other Professional Elite

Include them only if they are very exceptional. Heavily edit for key phrases.

Personal Interests

Tread thoughtfully here. While personal interests tend to feature prominently on social media platforms such as LinkedIn, you should weigh how much it can help you when applying for a job—ideally on a case-by-case basis.

It you include a section like this, keep the following in mind:

- **Advantages:** Personal interests can indicate a skill or area of knowledge that is related to the goal, such as photography for someone in public relations, or carpentry and wood-working for someone in construction management.

This section can show well-roundedness, good physical health, or knowledge of a subject related to the goal. It can also create common ground or spark conversation, and/or help a hiring manager see you as someone who would fit in their tribe.

- **Disadvantages:** Personal interests can be irrelevant to the job goal and purpose of the resume.

Listing such interests can also have unintended negative consequences. For example, if you're highly athletic and the people interviewing you aren't physically fit – or perhaps even self-conscious about that – the fact that you're super-fit might not play in your favour.

If in doubt, do not include a Personal Interests section.

Your reason for including it is most likely that you want to tell them about you. But, as you know, this is an ad. You are advertising yourself.

If this section would move the employer to understand why you would be the best candidate, include it; otherwise, forget about it.

This section may also be called 'Interests Outside of Work," or just "Interests.'

~

IN THE NEXT CHAPTER, WE LOOK AT HOW TO USE KEYWORDS TO GET your resume noticed.

"WORK IS EFFORT APPLIED TOWARD SOME END. THE MOST SATISFYING work involves directing our efforts toward achieving ends that we ourselves endorse as worthy expressions of our talent and character." — William J. Bennett

"YOU HAVE TO DO MORE THAN YOU GET PAID FOR BECAUSE THAT'S where the fortune is." — Jim Rohn

"DEFINE YOUR GOALS IN TERMS OF THE ACTIVITIES NECESSARY TO achieve them, and concentrate on those activities." — Brian Tracy

"DEVELOP AND MAINTAIN MOMENTUM BY WORKING CONTINUOUSLY toward your sales goals every day." — Brian Tracy

10. USING KEYWORDS IN YOUR RESUMÉ

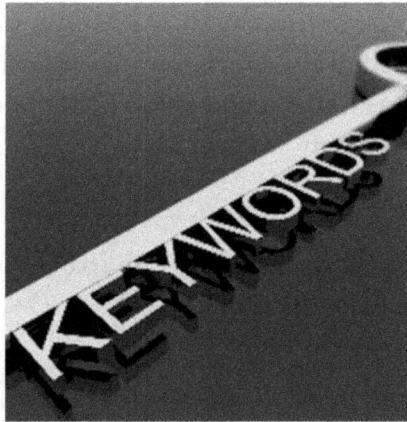

Using keywords in your resumé is similar to using keywords when creating a website or writing a blog. The purpose there is to make it easy for the search engines to index it and post the results. With your resume, keywords will help position you as a possible applicant for further attention.

Employers *do not* read every word on each resumé.

Keywords describe skills and qualifications. You might see them in the job posting you are answering and on related companies' websites. It would be useful to carefully scan the job posting to see if any keywords pop out for you. Then you can enhance your resumé by using as many keywords as you can.

But, do not make up experiences, just to use keywords.

$\sim$

IN THE NEXT CHAPTER, WE LOOK AT HOW TO MARKET YOUR transferable skills.

START BY DOING WHAT'S NECESSARY; THEN DO WHAT'S POSSIBLE; AND suddenly you are doing the impossible. — St. Francis of Assisi

"OPPORTUNITY IS LIKE A GOLD MINE... IF YOU DON'T PICK UP THE shovel, then you will be living in someone else's shaft." — Doug Firebaugh

"WE ARE CONTINUALLY FACED BY GREAT OPPORTUNITIES BRILLIANTLY disguised as insoluble problems." — Lee Iococca

"ARE YOU MISSING OPPORTUNITIES BECAUSE YOU ARE TOO FOCUSED ON obstacles?" — Jeffrey Gitomer

"SPEND 80 PERCENT OF YOUR TIME FOCUSING ON THE OPPORTUNITIES OF tomorrow rather than the problems of yesterday." — Brian Tracy

11. MARKETING YOUR TRANSFERRABLE SKILLS

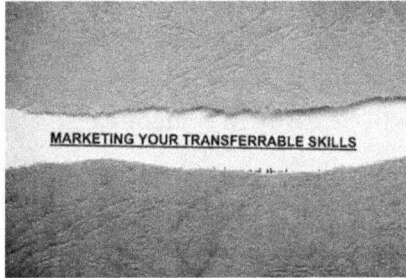

MARKETING YOUR TRANSFERRABLE SKILLS

Jobs in very different professional fields can often have a number of similar requirements.

Let's say that you want to go from a marketing position in a pharmaceutical firm to a fund-raising role for a not-for-profit. What are the skills you've already demonstrated that are applicable?

They may be more than you think.

Consider these possibilities:

- Time management

46

- Project management
- Collaboration
- Persuasive communicating
- Strong decision-making
- Innovative problem-solving
- Composure under pressure

Brainstorm a list of skills you have developed from different jobs that you have had in the past and see if any of them are transferrable to the job you are applying for now.

~

IN THE NEXT CHAPTER, WE LOOK AT USING *ACTION WORDS* TO MAXIMIZE your resume's content.

ABILITY IS WHAT YOU'RE CAPABLE OF DOING. MOTIVATION DETERMINES what you do. Attitude determines how well you do it. — Lou Holtz

"IF YOU ARE DOING YOUR BEST, YOU WILL NOT HAVE TO WORRY ABOUT failure." — Robert S. Hillyer

NEVER LET THE FEAR OF STRIKING OUT GET IN YOUR WAY. – BABE Ruth, 1895-1948, American Baseball Player

12. USING ACTION-ORIENTED WORDS

C losely tied to your use of correct grammar and formatting is the use of action-oriented words rather than passive ones.

But what are they?

Action verbs are verbs that will get noticed more and that will clearly communicate what your experience or achievements were.

Action verbs *imply* that you *actively* got things done. Examples include *managed, coached, enforced* and *planned*.

Look at everything you've written in your resume and add action verbs wherever possible. If you are reworking an existing resume, change any passive words to active language.

Here is a list of what some might call Power Words.

POWER WORDS

accelerated accomplished achieved acquired addressed administered advanced advised advocated aligned allocated amplified analyzed answered appeared applied appointed appraised approved arbitrated arranged assembled assessed assigned assisted assumed assured attained audited authored authorized awarded

blocked boosted bought briefed broadened brought budgeted built

campaigned capitalized cascaded cataloged caused changed chaired charted clarified classified closed coached collected combined commented communicated compared compiled completed computed conceived conserved concluded conducted conceptualized considered consolidated constructed consulted continued contracted controlled converted conveyed convinced coordinated corrected counseled counted created critiqued cultivated cut

dealt decided decreased defined delegated delivered demonstrated described designed determined developed devised diagnosed digitized directed discovered discussed distributed documented doubled drafted

earned edited educated effected elevated eliminated endorsed enforced engineered enhanced enlarged enlisted ensured entered established estimated evaluated examined exceeded executed expanded expedited experienced experimented explained explored expressed extended facilitated filed filled financed focused forecast forged formulated fostered found founded

gained gathered generated graded granted guided

halved handled headed up helped hired

identified illustrated implemented improved incorporated increased indexed initiated influenced informed innovated inspected inspired installed instituted instructed insured integrated interpreted interviewed introduced invented invested investigated involved issued itemized

joined

kept

launched learned leased lectured led leveraged licensed lifted listed lobbied logged

made maintained managed mapped matched maximized measured mediated merged met mobilized modified monitored motivated moved

named navigated negotiated

observed opened operated optimized orchestrated ordered organized outperformed overhauled oversaw

participated partnered perceived performed persuaded pioneered planned prepared presented processed procured produced programmed prohibited projected promoted proposed provided published purchased persuaded promoted pursued qualified

qualified quantified questioned

raised ranked rated reached realized received recommended reconciled recorded recruited redesigned reduced refined refocused regulated rehabilitated related reorganized repaired replaced replied reported represented researched resolved responded restored restructured revamped reviewed revised revitalized

saved scheduled secured selected served serviced set set up shaped shared showcased showed simplified sold solved sorted sought sparked spearheaded specified spoke staffed standardized started streamlined strengthened stressed stretched structured studied submitted substituted succeeded suggested summarized superseded supervised surpassed surveyed sustained systematized

tackled targeted taught terminated tested took toured traced tracked traded trained transferred transcribed transformed translated transported traveled treated trimmed tripled turned tutored

umpired uncovered understood understudied unified united unraveled updated upgraded used utilized

verbalized verified visited

waged weighed widened won worked wrote

yielded

13. REFERENCES INTRODUCTION

This is another one of those areas of the job searching process that have been modernized.

Where it was once appropriate to write 'references available upon request', it is now considered to be bad form. For one thing, you are stating the obvious. Of course, they are!

Asking and checking out your references is part of the hiring process should you be successful in your interview. Even more of a no-no is providing your references names and contact info as part of your resume.

If the employer has access to your references, they may just contact them before talking to you. That in turn prevents you from giving your contacts a heads up to tell them that a potential employer may be contacting them to learn more about you. You want your references to be ready to act as a cheerleader on your behalf.

∾

IN THE NEXT CHAPTER, WE INTRODUCE THE IDEA OF BRANDING YOUR resume.

"IF YOU AREN'T FIRED WITH ENTHUSIASM, YOU WILL BE FIRED WITH enthusiasm." — Vince Lombardi

"DOING WHAT WE WERE MEANT TO DO CREATES FUN, EXCITEMENT AND contentment in our lives, and invariably, in the lives of the people around us. When you're excited about something it's contagious." — Mark Victor Hansen

GET EXCITED AND ENTHUSIASTIC ABOUT YOUR OWN DREAM. THIS excitement is like a forest fire — you can smell it, taste it, and see it from a mile away. —Denis Waitley

"WHEN THERE'S HOPE IN THE FUTURE THERE'S POWER IN THE PRESENT." — John Maxwell

14. BRANDING YOUR RESUMÉ

I'm a strong proponent of personal marketing and promotion, blowing your own horn, so to speak. I believe business professionals should market themselves in a professional way.

Where businesses have branded their products and services for years, this practice has carried over to personal branding. Some would tell you that this is the way to go when job searching to ensure you stand out from all the other applicants.

I'm not going to tell you that this is the definite way to go, but I will give you some info on the topic and you can decide for yourself.

One suggestion might be to create a *so-called* normal resumé as well as a branded one. You could try using each of them and see what happens.

To start with, develop a personal branding or value proposition statement and use it on your resumé, cover letters, interviews, networking and all job-related communications, including social networking activities.

When it comes to personal branding, all branding for that matter, it is important that you are consistent in all areas.

A personal branding statement or value proposition is similar to what is often called a USP (Universal Sales Proposition) in the business world. It is a short tagline that encapsulates how you *differentiate* yourself from others.

This can take some time to develop and you will want to test it on friends and colleagues to see if it works for you. You don't want to come across as being cheesy or boastful.

Please locate and read the ***Developing your USP*** document. It's available in the Resources section at the end of this book.

We talked earlier about how *Career Objective Statements* are a thing of the past. Some resumé writers believe the strategy of using a profile summary or *career summary* is now also history.

Instead, they suggest it should include a ***personal-brand snapshot***.

The idea is that you give the reader *newsworthy information* in *short, effective statements* so they can get the facts and move on.

This reason is *exactly* why newspapers and news articles start with a great headline, give the most critical facts/details first, and then gradually fill in the not-so-critical details further down in the story. They know you want the important information first and don't want to wait for it.

Those same resumé writers advise doing the same in your resumé.

Start with your branding statement and make it answer the decision maker's questions:

"Why should I care?" or

"What's in it for me?"

When time is of the essence, answering these questions first gives readers exactly what they need to know up front; then they can choose to keep on reading for any details.

Corporate branding marketers utilize certain colours to emphasize their brand. The same applies to developing your personal brand. Certain colors may have specific meanings to *you* and can be used to develop your personal brand!

With ever-decreasing attention spans, some resumé writers are suggesting writing tweet-sized resumé sentences as a sound strategy. And this doesn't seem to be a trend that is fading away in the coming years either.

The next time you write a sentence for your resumé, see how many characters are included. And then see if you can get it down to 140 characters or fewer without losing impact.

Consider what is *essential* and what is *critical*.

Ditch the *essential* and run with the *critical*.

$\sim$

IN THE NEXT CHAPTER, WE LOOK AT LEVERAGING YOUR DIGITAL MEDIA footprint.

"DRESS FOR SUCCESS. IMAGE IS VERY IMPORTANT. PEOPLE JUDGE YOU BY the way you look on the outside." — Brian Tracy

15. LEVERAGING YOUR DIGITAL FOOTPRINT/USING SOCIAL MEDIA

R esumés, used to function as your 'first impression' to an employer.

In some industries, things are *rapidly changing*. They are now *quickly becoming* the second or third thing an employer may see about you.

With the rise of social media sites such as LinkedIn, website resumés, portfolios, video resumés, and job-search strategies that allow job seekers to tap into the hidden job market and bypass sending a resumé as a first introduction, the human eye is quickly becoming the #1 gatekeeper.

Employers may be *looking* for you, or someone like you, to fill a vacancy, using the very same social media tools, such as Facebook, Twitter and blogs. If you are on-line and you have your keywords highlighted to resonate with those that an employer would be looking for, there is a good chance that you will be discovered.

This is even before the employer has seen your resume.

FIRST IMPRESSIONS ARE IMPORTANT - IF YOU DON'T WANT A POTENTIAL employer to see something, don't make it publicly accessible or put it online at all.

LET'S LOOK AT *LEVERAGING* YOUR ON-LINE PRESENCE, OFTEN CALLED your digital footprint. You can use social media to your advantage. Remember that you're marketing yourself.

Owning your digital footprint is also about taking advantage of an additional opportunity to make a good impression. Here lays the challenge. Not everybody is on-line.

Staying off the grid on social media can work against you. While you may want to keep your private and professional lives separate, having such high privacy settings that no one can find you online, or being offline altogether, can hurt your chances during a job search.

93% of employers say they screen candidates on social media before hiring them and **if** they can't find any mention of you online, it's a red flag. They could very well interpret it as you have something to hide... or that you're simply not very technologically savvy and not using the latest communication tools.

SO, ASSUMING, THAT YOU ARE ON-LINE, HOW DO YOU LEVERAGE YOUR on-line presence?

One way is to utilize your social profiles in a way that will confirm what employers want to see. The most common websites for recruiters to screen candidates on are LinkedIn, Twitter and Facebook. What you post and how you behave on these sites can create a first impression of the sort of person you might be or want to be seen as.

Employers look at your profiles to see if they can find out more about your qualifications, to see if you are creative and to see if you'll be a good fit with their team. They'll also be watching for red flags such as poor grammar and spelling, anti-social behaviour, or anger issues.

This doesn't mean linking potential employers to your Facebook photo albums so your prospective new boss can see how fun you are when you go on vacation or having a good time at a party.

This means linking your LinkedIn profile (and if you don't have one yet, you should get one--the basic version is free) to your resumé and making sure they match.

When Linkedin first came on the scene, it was very much like having your resumé on steroids.

Now, it is very similar to the new way that we are using for resumé writing. You don't want to just copy and paste your resumé on your LinkedIn profile.

However, you should spend some time updating it so that your Linkedin profile generally contains the same job history and responsibilities as your resumé does. They should work together to promote you as an ideal job candidate.

Your Linkedin profile allows you to expand a little upon some of the details that you used in your resumé. Linkedin can also be a good venue for posting testimonials from people you have worked within the past.

Be sure to ask people to provide recommendations for you, in particular those people who can speak to the strengths that you most want to be emphasized. These aren't the same as references, however some of the glowing testimonials may very well serve as a source of references for you.

Be sure any e-mail addresses and social media handles shared are appropriate that is... unprofessional looking. If you have identified in your resume publications or articles you have written, your Linkedin profile can be a great place to highlight them.

Don't forget that you should also have a recent photo on your LinkedIn profile and while it can be candid, it should also have an air of professionalism about it.

Besides Linkedin, other social media venues offer valuable possibilities for powering your job search, as well as a few potential downsides. Be sure your digital footprint is an asset as you prepare your resumé.

Make sure you own your digital footprint.

Social media is a primarily a vehicle for communication. You will want to include at least one of your social media accounts on your resumé. As I mentioned earlier, be sure that any e-mail addresses and social media profile names look and sound professional. If not, create new ones.

Understand that most employers – 65% or more – use social networks to research candidates. Roughly half of them do so to see if the candidate is likely to be a 'good fit' for their culture – in other words, right for their tribe.

It is documented that employers regularly review social media to see if there are reasons *not* to hire an applicant. So, it is imperative you review all your social media postings and clean up any content that you wouldn't want a prospective employer to see.

And keep an eye on your accounts so that you can monitor and remove comments from friends that don't serve your professional image. Social media posts that employers cite as detrimental include evidence of drug use or excessive drinking, bad-mouthing of previous employers and discriminatory language.

Being active on social media can advance your professional interests and possibilities. Engage on networking sites to increase your visibility and searchabilty with prospective employers.

And while you're active on social media, to accommodate search engines, be sure you are using a consistent version of your professional name. If you're "Robert A. Jones" on Linkedin, you should be Robert A. Jones in your resume and on your other social media accounts – not Rob Jones here and there. Your professional 'screen name' is probably your most important keyword especially for search engine generated results.

Let's look at using social media and on-line resources for job searching.

You can find lots of valuable information on-line about a potential employer, if you are willing to spend some time researching.

And you should!

As mentioned, follow your prospective employer on Linkedin, Twitter, Facebook, Instagram, and any other social media platform they may use. Don't forget their company website! Think of what you see as an aggregated news feed about the employer.

It doesn't take long to begin to get a real sense of the organization's culture, values, and work environment intel that can help you prepare the most thoughtful resume possible – and it can also help you immensely as you later prepare for an interview.

- Make sure that you have cleaned up your own social media profile, if necessary.

- What is their history?

- What do they emphasize in their messaging?

- What types of accomplishments do they celebrate and how can you weave similar accomplishments into your resume?

- What kind of language do they use to describe achievements?

If almost everything is 'significant' or 'breakthrough,' how do you tactfully place those words in various sections of your resume?

- Who are the decision makers?

- What is their hiring philosophy?

- What kind of work culture is it?

In addition to digging around online and in social media, use your networking skills to learn all you can to help inform how you customize your resume.

Do all the research you can, from on-line searches and social media tracking to networking with people you know. If you know anyone who works there, approach them for a conversation – or better yet, coffee or lunch.

Research shows that your resumé must demonstrate that you have at least 70% of a job's requirements to have a legitimate hope of landing an interview. And bear in mind that one of the advantages of social media is that you can gain access to people you otherwise might not.

Search for someone within your connections who is connected to a person of interest to you. Perhaps they are in the field in which you are seeking work; perhaps they work for a company you wish to get in to – then ask your contact to introduce you.

You can leverage your research results to tweak your Skills and Accomplishments section of your resume. When customizing your resumé for a specific position, take careful note of the skills required and use any number of those words in your resume.

If you think of yourself as someone who 'leads stakeholder communications,' but the employer uses the phrase 'stakeholder engagement' – that's right, you're now an expert in stakeholder engagement.

If you have 'increased website and social media traffic' in your current job, but your prospective employer's website discusses 'online presence' – your resumé should note that you 'elevated online presence.'

The big caveat of course, is that you really do have those skills.

~

OUR NEXT CHAPTER IS SPECIFIC TO PROFESSIONALS WHO HAVE BEEN using a curriculum vitae to search for a job.

"IF YOU THINK YOU CAN DO A THING OR THAT YOU CANNOT DO A THING, in either case you are right." — Henry Ford

"START BY DOING WHAT'S NECESSARY; THEN DO WHAT'S POSSIBLE; AND suddenly you are doing the impossible." — St. Francis of Assisi

"I USED TO SAY, 'I SURE HOPE THINGS WILL CHANGE.' THEN I LEARNED that the only way things are going to change for me is when I change." — Jim Rohn

"CONSULT NOT YOUR FEARS BUT YOUR HOPES AND YOUR DREAMS. THINK not about your frustrations, but about your unfulfilled potential. Concern yourself not with what you tried and failed in, but with what it is still possible for you to do." — Pope John XXIII

"IF YOU BELIEVE IN WHAT YOU ARE DOING, THEN LET NOTHING HOLD YOU up in your work. Much of the best work of the world has been done against seeming impossibilities. The thing is to get the work done." — Dale Carnegie

16. CV TO RESUMÉ

A Curriculum Vitae (CV) is mainly for professors, teachers, lawyers, scientists and related professionals. At least in North America it is. I understand that the term CV is used interchangeably with that of resume in other parts of the world.

This chapter is directed at professionals that use a Curriculum Vitae, which is basically a story of the professional life.

Academics may have 10- or 12-page-long CVs, or even more.

The downside with so much information is that *often*, some of their most impressive experiences get lost on page six or seven. You need to get to the point! It is recommended that you highlight your most notable achievements on one page.

The goal is to get a hiring manager to get excited about you and what you bring to the table. If the manager likes what they see, they of course can then read through your entire CV.

So, short version, change your CV to a résumé.

Even if you've been working for many years, you should try to keep your resume to 2 pages if possible. And don't throw out that CV. Some job postings may ask for either. Be prepared!

∽

"THERE ARE TWO WAYS OF MEETING DIFFICULTIES. YOU ALTER THE difficulties or you alter yourself to meet them." — Phyllis Bottome

"AFTER EVERY DIFFICULTY, ASK YOURSELF TWO QUESTIONS: 'WHAT DID I do right?' and 'What would I do differently?'— Brian Tracy

"ATTITUDE, HUMOR AND ACTION (PERSISTENCE) WILL WHIP FEARS AND rejection. Fear of failure doesn't exist, if you believe it doesn't." — Jeffrey Gitomer

"DON'T LET MINOR SETBACKS CLOUD YOUR VISION OF THE FUTURE. BE like Captain James Cook, the famous English explorer. He faced monumental obstacles, but he kept sailing on. Said the captain, 'I had ambition not only to go farther than any man had ever been before, but as far as it was possible for a man to go.'"— Neil Eskelin

17. ADDITIONAL RESOURCES

Here is a collection of job interview preparation related questions asked on Quora.com and answered by me, Rae Stonehouse.

It's cumbersome to add hyperlinks in this printed version, so I haven't.

If you would like to read more answers to the questions, from people who may or may not agree with me... and some... who may be from outer space and worth a chuckle, just visit Quora and enter the title of the question into their search bar.

~

18. DEVELOPING YOUR USP

Your USP:

Your **unique selling proposition** (a.k.a. **unique selling point**, universal selling point or **USP**) is a marketing concept used to differentiate yourself from your competitors or others in the market place.

Some good current examples of products with a clear USP are:

- Head & Shoulders: "You get rid of dandruff"

Some unique propositions that were pioneers when they were introduced:

- Domino's Pizza: "You get fresh, hot pizza delivered to your door in 30 minutes or less—or it's free."
- FedEx: "When your package absolutely, positively has to get there overnight"
- M&M's: "Melts in your mouth, not in your hand"
- Metropolitan Life: "Get Met, It Pays"

The term USP has been largely replaced by the concept of a *Positioning Statement*. Positioning is determining what place a brand (tan-

68

gible good or service) should occupy in the consumer's mind in comparison to its competition. A position is often described as the meaningful difference between the brand and its competitors.
Source: Wikipedia

I recently was blindsided at a Chamber of Commerce function in my city when we were standing in circle participating in what they call a power networking session. We were asked what makes us or our business unique. I didn't recognize it as a USP question and provided an ineffective response. If I had recognized it for what it was i.e. a USP question I would have responded with "Mr. Emcee is a full-service event organizer. From start to finish ... we do it all!"

Your challenge is to develop a USP that on one hand is short and to the point, yet is clear enough that it captures the essence of your business and will stick in the mind of whoever you are sharing it with. Having it prepared in advance, believing in it and being able to recite it with a moment's notice will go a long way in reducing your anxiety and fear which are all part of shyness.

I would also suggest researching your competitors or others that are in a similar business that are not necessarily your competitors to see if they have chosen a similar USP as you have. I am aware of two business coaches that chose a USP that had only one word that was different. That one word totally changed the context of the USP but it really upset one of the coaches accusing the other of stealing her idea, even though they had been developed independent of each other.

Power Networking Logistics:

1. Research your competitors to learn what their USPs are.
2. Create a USP for your business.
3. Share it with colleagues and ask their opinion. Ask if it makes sense. Ask if it is easy to understand. Ask if it captures the essence of your business.

WHAT DO YOU STAND FOR?

WHAT IS YOUR USP?

~

19. QUESTION: SHOULD I ADD TEMP & CONTRACTOR POSITION TO LINKEDIN & MY RESUME?

Answer Provided:

I don't think it is so much as doing it a proper way as it is doing it an 'effective' way.

Working as a contractor or a temp, are two very different situations.

As a consultant, you are an independent contractor. You are not an employee of the client. You provide specific work for the client. In this case, you would be well-advised to seek permission from past and current clients to be able to publicly post their name. They may not want it known that they have engaged the services of a consultant. Gaining permission to promote your connection to a company may be something that you want to address as a term in your beginning contract or proposal.

You can still promote yourself as a consultant and describe the type of services that you provide without actually mentioning your current client by name. Once you have completed your contract, see if you can get them to write a testimonial for you. If they do so, this would seem to imply that you would be able to mention their business by name.

Working as a temp would seem to indicate that you are currently working for an Employment/Temp agency that has placed you at a worksite that they have contracted with. Your employer is actually the Temp agency and not the worksite.

I would start off by stating the name of the Temp Agency you are working for. In your description of your experience you could add one or more of the businesses you have worked for and add some details as to the work you did there and the skills that you developed.

The fact that you are a temp, shouldn't make a difference. Work is work.

~

20. QUESTION: WHAT IS THE BEST FORMAT TO INCLUDE A PROFESSIONAL INTERNATIONAL ASSIGNMENT ON A RESUME? (ENGINEERING ASSIGNMENT IN JAPAN FOR 6 MONTHS)

Answer Provided:

How you proceed is likely determined by whether your international assignment is part of your overall, i.e. additional experience, or your sole experience.

I would start off by taking a close look at what your duties in the assignment were. Cross-index them with the specific job description you worked under if you still have access.

Brainstorm a list of duties & skills that you were required to use in the position. Create a separate file with all your brainstormed items.

Any position that you apply for should have a resume specifically created for it.

Taking a close look at the job description and its requirements, look to see what skills and experience you have that meets the job description.

It has been said that if you meet at least 70% of the requirements, you are likely to get an interview.

Take your newly crafted and highlighted skills & experience and add them to your Experience section. You want the employer/hiring manager to quickly see that you have the right stuff for the position and are worthy of an interview.

You should also craft your opening Summary Statement so that it highlights your experience as a worthy candidate for the position.

Good luck in your job search!

As answered on Quora.com.

~

21. QUESTION: WHAT CAN I DO IF MY BOSS CAN'T GIVE ME A REFERENCE?

My boss at my last job of many years is contractually forbidden to give me a reference for my job search, other than confirming my dates of service. How should I handle that in my resume and in interviews?

Answer Provided:

I see providing your boss as a reference for your current job searching as a wasted opportunity. If the new employer is checking you out, they are likely to contact your former boss anyways. And yes, they are limited to what they can say about you.

You would be far better off in creating better references. These are people you have worked with. They may be work colleagues, customers, clients and/or other supervisors.

The idea is that they are in position as your cheerleader. They know what and how you did at work and they are willing to promote you for the job in hand.

They need to be in communication with you. As your resume should be crafted for a specific job opportunity, your references should also be specific. You can develop a list of references and pick and choose from your list depending on their credibility in relation to the job you are applying for.

Your references have no place in your resume. And don't say "references are available upon request." Of course they are!

I can't see how your current boss not giving you a reference would come up in an interview, other than perhaps in a question like "What would your former boss say about your ability to do your job?" This gives you an opportunity to promote yourself, using your boss's words, which you have made up of course.

As answered on Quora.com.

22. QUESTION: HOW SHOULD YOU LIST SAME JOB TITLE IN THE SAME COMPANY BUT DIFFERENT DEPARTMENTS ON YOUR RESUME?

Answer Provided:

This question seems to have been kicking around for a while, but hopefully my response will help anyone pondering the same question.

I would suggest separating the two jobs. They were two different jobs, just happening to have the same title.

I would list it as the 'Job Title/Position' 'Department' 'Years i.e. start/end'.

This would allow you to expand a little upon the slight differences in each position.

As for the company wanting to hire you now, they have already seen your resume. I don't see any need to say anything, as it may make you look unsure of yourself.

If the interviewer is curious about the two jobs being lumped together, they are likely to ask you about it. Be prepared to answer how the two similar jobs came to be.

As originally answered on Quora.com.

~

WHEN YOU WANT SOMETHING BADLY ENOUGH, YOU WILL DEVELOP THE confidence and the ability to overcome any obstacle in your way. — Brian Tracy

"WANTING SOMETHING IS NOT ENOUGH. YOU MUST HUNGER FOR IT. Your motivation must be absolutely compelling in order to overcome the obstacles that will invariably come your way." — Les Brown

IT'S NEVER TOO LATE TO REALIZE YOUR AMBITIONS. TAKE THE FIRST step by daring to dream big dreams. Then have the confidence to take a few risks and make those dreams a reality. You'll be glad you did. — Don MacRae, President of the Lachlan Group

"DON'T GET COMPLACENT. PUSH YOURSELF OUT OF YOU COMFORT ZONE and set higher standards of achievement for yourself. Once you've achieved a standard of excellence, never let it rest--push yourself even higher." — Dave Anderson

"IDENTIFY AND DEVELOP YOUR UNIQUE TALENTS AND ABILITIES, THE things that make you special." — Brian Tracy

23. QUESTION: IN A COVER LETTER, IS IT OK TO SAY "THANK YOU FOR YOUR DISCRETION" TO AVOID THEM FROM CONTACTING CURRENT EMPLOYERS?

Answer Provided:

I had to give some thought to this question.

Your cover letter is presumably written to accompany your resume and perhaps an application form, in anticipation to being invited for an interview.

I don't see why they would want to contact your current employer at this stage of the game as they haven't even met you yet. So, I would say don't add 'thank you for your discretion.'

If you make it to the interview stage, you are going to need to be prepared for the fact that they very well may contact your current employer.

Some will make the offer, contingent upon contacting your references.

Some may want to do some preliminary research on you prior to making an offer.

If you make it this far, you will need to be prepared for your current employer being contacted. Might be a good idea to advise them in advance that you are looking for another job.

As originally answered on Quora.com.

～

24. QUESTION: IN APPLYING TO DIRECTOR-LEVEL "MBA" TYPE JOBS, HOW MUCH TIME SHOULD IT BE TAKING ME TO CUSTOMIZE MY RESUME BULLETS AND COVER LETTER?

Answer Provided:

It'll take as much time as it takes to do so...

In creating a resume, if you haven't already, there is value in brainstorming a list of duties and responsibilities that you have had with each of your positions. This would go into your resume data file.

When you are customizing your resume, you need to take these generated duties & responsibilities and rework the wording on them tying them into the requirements of the job requirements.

That would likely mean that your resume would be substantially different for each position you apply for.

Your resume should be a dynamic tool i.e. it is always being changed to meet the requirements of a specific job.

As for the cover letter, there are likely elements such as the opening and the closing that can be reused for different applications, but the so-called meat and potatoes i.e. the body of the letter should be customized for each position.

$\sim$

25. QUESTION: WHAT DO YOU PUT IN A RESUME FOR AN INTROVERT WHO HASN'T DONE MUCH SOCIAL STUFF IN SCHOOL?

Answer Provided:

The fact that you are a self-proclaimed introvert, is irrelevant when it comes to creating your resume.

You also claim to be shy i.e. 'hasn't done much social stuff in school' doesn't get reflected in your resume but certainly will when you start applying for jobs and going for job interviews.

You don't say what field you will be applying for jobs in, if any specifically. I'm also assuming that this may be your first job in the working world and you likely don't have a vast amount of work experience to draw upon.

We all had to start somewhere. Everybody has a first job. It may not be exactly what you are looking for, but it can be a stepping stone to bigger and better jobs.

The fact that you are shy may be an obstacle in performing the duties of the job if the employer has the expectation that the new hire is an outgoing person.

There are many jobs out there that fit the needs of introverts, or where introversion or extraversion doesn't matter. You may have to do some research to find one.

Assuming you are over the age of 18, I would recommend that you research to see if there is a Toastmasters club in your community. Joining one will help you develop your communication & leadership skills, which in turn will help increase your self-confidence. A Toastmasters club also provides ample opportunities to hone your socialization skills with fellow members of all ages.

There can be an added benefit of working on projects or tasks that can add some substance to your resume. In the beginning, every little bit can help.

As originally answered on Quora.com.

～

26. QUESTION: HOW CAN I WRITE A GOOD CV FOR A JOB WHEN I HAVE NO WORK EXPERIENCE?

Answer Provided:

You have a challenge before you, but no different than anyone else that graduates from school then goes looking for work in their chosen field.

Others have done it and you will as well.

Looking for work is work... and you have some work ahead of you.

In my part of the world, western Canada, we call a CV a resume, so I will refer to it as such from now on.

From your Bio, it looks like you have a Bachelor of Science in Economics & Banking.

Assuming this is the field that you are looking for work in, you have several strategies that you need to be undertaking, simultaneously.

1. **Creating your resume:** A well-crafted resume helps you get an interview. Wowing the Interviewer in the job interview gets you the job.
2. **Researching the job market:** Having graduated fairly recently and not having a current job to leverage, you will

likely be looking at an entry-level job to start or to get your foot in the door, so to speak. I would suggest researching all of the jobs in your field that are available locally, in your own country and abroad. This helps to give you an idea of what kinds of jobs are out there and what they are looking for in ways of skills and experience. Your research should also provide you with 'buzz' words or words/terminology that are used in your industry. These can be helpful when creating the content for your resume.

3. **Reviewing your educational experience:** You likely have a wealth of skills that you have developed in your education. These are marketable. In addition, you will have skills that are considered to be transferrable i.e. if they are usable in one situation, they are likely usable in others. Then there are your soft skills. Examples of these are having good people skills, work ethic, communicating skills including being a good listener etc. You won't necessarily add these to your resume, but it will be helpful when you get to your interview. So, make a list under these three headings and brainstorm all the skills that you possess under each heading.

4. **Linkedin?** If not, you should be! Your resume and your Linkedin profile should resonate, that is that they should support each other. Your resume needs to be crafted rather terse and succinct. Whereas, your Linkedin profile allows you to expand upon some of the items that you have highlighted on your resume.

5. **References:** As you don't have work experience to draw upon, you will need to leverage your connections from your school experience. This could include professors, fellow students or perhaps supervisors from school/work projects.

6. **Volunteer Work:** If you haven't already, I would suggest finding some volunteer work in your field. Financial literacy is one subject that comes to mind. There are usually opportunities available with not for profit organizations that help others with their financial knowledge.

NOW BACK TO YOUR RESUME, I HAVEN'T FORGOTTEN ABOUT IT.

There are different formats out there, but most follow a basic flow. Starting off with a strong Summary Statement. A Summary Statement can help you customize your resumé for different opportunities. This is especially helpful if your background is somewhat general, as is yours at this point. You can use your summary statement to highlight skills and experience most relevant for each position.

Every job that you apply for should have a specifically crafted summary statement targeting the requirements of the job and featuring you as an ideal candidate.

Next in your resume would be your experience. As you don't have any work experience, you will need to use the content that you generated from the previous brain-storming exercise.

I read somewhere that if you have 70% of the requirements for a specific job, you are likely to get an interview. This translates to the fact that if you do get called for an interview, then they must think you are worthy of consideration. During the interview, you need to wow them. They know that you are entering the workforce. Your task is to convince them that you are eager to learn and will do your best in the new role.

Good luck in your job search journey.

For more sage advice on job searching and landing your dream job, visit http://yourehirednow.com

To keep up to date on what is trending in the job searching field, Like us and Follow us on Facebook. Job Search Strategies That Work.

∼

27. QUESTION: WHAT IS THE BEST WAY TO WRITE A DYNAMIC COVER LETTER?

Answer Provided:

'Dynamic' is likely a subjective term. For hiring agents, who likely receive volumes of cover letters, 'dynamic' may not be a term they use.

I would suspect that they are looking for a cover letter that indicates the candidate is truly interested in the available job, they have researched the organization, they are qualified and experienced to take on the position and they actually are available.

With that in mind, like creating a good speech/presentation, I would suggest that you start at the end.

Your conclusion is where you determine what it is you want to leave your reader with. Presumably, it would be to encourage the Hiring Manager to actually read your resume and then to invite you in for an interview where you can impress upon them in person.

Too many people make the mistake of asking for the job in their cover letter. Save that for after the interview.

You should spend some time crafting your Summary Statement for your resume. Your Summary Statement should be prominently featured in your Cover Letter, with an abbreviated version of content from your resume to attract the reader's attention. The idea is that you grab their interest, they then check out your resume for more details.

Your Summary Statement on your resume should be consistent with your Linkedin profile, where you can provide more details or proof of what you say that you can do. If a Hiring Manager is interested in you, they will most certainly check out your digital footprint e.g. social media.

A big thing to remember with your Summary Statement is that you need to craft your content from the perspective that you are a solution to the Hiring Manager's problem. You need to feature what you can do, not what you have done. To expand upon that a little, you can leverage your past experience to give you credence for what you can do in the future.

Keep your cover letter short at a page or a little more.

Your cover letter needs to be crafted specifically for the position and organization you are applying for. You can reuse much of your content, but it needs to be tweaked for each occasion.

Your cover letter needs to be addressed to the person who is most likely to read it. With the amount of applications that are being requested to be submitted on line, your cover letter may just get to an HR manager, where it is likely to be chucked out and not to the person who should be getting it.

~

28. QUESTION: IF A JOB ASKS FOR A COVER LETTER AND YOU DON'T HAVE ONE, YET YOU ANSWER ALL THEIR QUESTIONS CORRECTLY, CAN YOU STILL GET THE JOB?

Answer Provided:

Possibly... possibly not!

A cover letter by itself isn't going to get you a job. When accompanied by a well-written resume, it sets up the possibility of being invited to be interviewed.

You mention that you have answered all their questions correctly. You are a little lean on details here. Was this on-line as part of an application process of some sort?

If you have already had an interview and the questions you refer to were part of the interview, I would be surprised if you actually did answer all of their questions correctly. For some questions, there are no right and wrong answers. The test is to see *how* you answer them.

And if you have already had an interview, worrying about a cover letter at this stage serves no purpose. They wouldn't have interviewed you if they didn't think you were a possible candidate.

I wouldn't expect that whether you get the job at this stage would matter at all based on the fact you didn't submit a cover letter.

Probably what is most important is 'what are you going to do next time that a job asks for a cover letter?'

∾

29. QUESTION: SHOULD I INCLUDE MY WORK ETHIC IN A COVER LETTER?

I usually dedicate 100 hours per week to work or projects as I love what I do and feel as if I'm not making good use of my time if I work less. I'm tossed between it coming off as fake and/or boastful vs. it being seen as a merit.

Answer Provided:

If you are defining your work ethic as regularly working 100 hours per week, I certainly wouldn't include it in a cover letter.

If you are a lawyer, perhaps, but otherwise, no way!

Working that many hours, if anything, illustrates that you do not have balance in your life. As well, working that many hours on a regular basis is not sustainable in the long run. A potential employer could look at your habit negatively and make an assumption that you could be leading to a breakdown, which could in turn cost them money.

Having worked in the mental health field most of my career, I can tell you that there is merit to the old saying of "all work and no play, makes Jack a dull boy!" It can also lead to mental health issues. We are meant to have leisure, recreational and pleasurable activities in our life. That's where the balance would come in.

If you feel the need to make it known that you regularly put in a lot of hours, you might be better off to have one of your job references make mention of the fact. Or you can have someone provide you a Linkedin testimonial attesting to the fact.

Highlighting that you are a workaholic in your cover letter would not be a good idea.

As answered on Quora.com.

~

IT'S NEVER TOO LATE TO REALIZE YOUR AMBITIONS. TAKE THE FIRST step by daring to dream big dreams. Then have the confidence to take a few risks and make those dreams a reality. You'll be glad you did. — Don MacRae, President of the Lachlan Group

"DON'T GET COMPLACENT. PUSH YOURSELF OUT OF YOU COMFORT ZONE and set higher standards of achievement for yourself. Once you've achieved a standard of excellence, never let it rest--push yourself even higher." — Dave Anderson

"IDENTIFY AND DEVELOP YOUR UNIQUE TALENTS AND ABILITIES, THE things that make you special." — Brian Tracy

30. QUESTION: IF WE FORGOT SOMETHING ON THE APPLICATION FORM, CAN WE PROVIDE A COVER LETTER TO ADD THE INFORMATION?

Answer Provided:

You could, but don't expect it to be of any benefit.

Let's assume that anyone actually reads your cover letter. I would expect that it wouldn't be appreciated. Reading your letter takes them away from something else they need to be doing. They also have to match your new information with your original submission. That takes more time. If there are hundreds of applications, your new information could be a nuisance.

You also don't want to give them the impression you are forgetful or not very well organized. If the new information is important enough to be mentioned… it should have been included in the first place.

I would suggest learning from this experience, so you can include it next time. If you do get an interview and the new info that you have is important enough to mention, do so. At that point, it might be of benefit.

As answered on Quora.com.

∿

31. QUESTION: WHAT IS GOOD ADDITIONAL INFORMATION TO LEAVE ON A RESUME?

Answer Provided:

This question is a little confusing to me in what it is asking.

Your resume should be crafted so all the information included, serves the purpose of marketing you as the best candidate for a specific job.

Your resume isn't a conversation with the reader i.e. the hiring manager. It is a snapshot illustrating the assets that you have to offer and proof you have done so.

The purpose of your resume is to pique the Hiring Manager's interest to invite you in for an interview.

If you have 'additional' information worth mentioning, this would be the place to share it.

Without knowing precisely what your additional information you are referring to is, you might be better adding it to a cover letter, when you submit your application.

However, don't assume that your cover letter will even be read. With applicant processing software present in many organizations, your cover letter may not be accepted, nor forwarded on to the appropriate hiring manager.

As answered on Quora.com.

~

32. QUESTION: SHOULD I PUT MY 3-MONTH SECONDMENT WITHIN THE SAME COMPANY ON MY RESUME AND LINKEDIN PROFILE? THE ROLE IS DIFFERENT AND IN A DIFFERENT COUNTRY.

Answer Provided:

Unless the seconded position was totally irrelevant to your career path and adds no value to your resume, I would add it to your resume and Linkedin profile.

Taking on a time-limited, seconded position can help show that you are flexible and willing to take on challenges.

Experience is experience. The trick is to leverage the skills you gained at the seconded position, to your regular position and hopefully, setting you up for a future position.

I would suggest taking the 'buzz' words from the seconded position's job duties and strategically add them to your resume, under the Experience Section.

Write them in past tense but action-oriented verbs e.g. created, developed, initiated, promoted etc.

As answered on Quora.com.

~

33. QUESTION: HOW DO I ADDRESS BEING FIRED FROM A PREVIOUS JOB IN A RESUME, ON AN APPLICATION, AND INTERVIEWS?

Answer Provided:

Unless the interviewer personally knows you, or knows of your situation, it isn't likely to come up in an interview, unless you draw attention to the fact.

If you are applying for work within the same company, likely there will be documentation on your personnel record.

The challenge is that you need to be *prepared* to explain an absence from the workforce, as identified in your resume, if it took you a while to get another job. Or if the one you are applying for is the next one since you got fired.

In the off chance that you are asked about your 'firing' you can minimalize its negative effect by having a story prepared in advance. The 'why' you got terminated may not be as important as what you learned from the situation.

The last time I got fired, I used the time to upgrade my skills in interpersonal conflict resolution, assertiveness and interpersonal communication. I became a stronger personality as a result of being fired.

Another aspect to address is how you feel about being fired. Being fired can shake you up for a while. The important thing I personally learned was that while the employer can take my job but they can't take my dignity. As you travel through life, you may very well get fired. It happens. But life goes on.

As answered on Quora.com.

~

34. QUESTION: CAN I ATTACH MY PORTFOLIO WITH MY COVER LETTER (AS THE FIRST DOCUMENT) IN THE SAME PDF DOCUMENT?

W hen applying to jobs in the creative industry, if my experience is less than others applying, but I have a killer portfolio, I want the hiring manager to see it right away, instead of viewing my resume/cover letter and then deciding if it's worth going on my portfolio website.

Answer Provided:

The only way to know for sure is to try it and see what happens.

If it works, do it again. If not, try something else.

You don't say what exactly it is that you do within the 'creative' industry. Whatever it is, it would likely be worth your while to use your best work in your cover letter/PDF or wherever, as bait, to encourage the hiring manager to go to the next level of checking out your portfolio website.

It's very much like fishing. They won't bite if they don't see anything interesting. Your task is to pique their interest, so they will bring you in for an interview.

If possible, whatever is that you highlight of your work, there should be some kind of a tie in to the job you are applying for. The idea is you want to be seen as the solution to their problem.

As answered on Quora.com.

∼

35. QUESTION: WHAT ARE THE VITAL AND PERSONAL INFORMATION THAT SHOULD NEVER BE DISCLOSED ON MY CV?

Answer Provided:

I don't believe that there are any hard and fast rules of what you shouldn't include, but here are some that I can think of.

1. Don't include your references contact info. If the employer has these in advance, they may contact them first and find no need to talk to you.

2. Don't say 'references available on request.' Of course they are!

3. SIN or Social Security Number. You will be asked for one after you are hired.

4. Don't quote your yearly wage from former positions.

5. Don't list absolutely everything you have ever done throughout your life. Pick the best and highlight it.

You ask about your CV. While many professional positions are asking for CVs, resumes are becoming the norm. Now it's not so much what you have done, as it is what you can do for the employer. Have you created a resume yet?

As answered on Quora.com.

36. QUESTION: HOW DO I BOOST MY CV AND GET A JOB FASTER?

Answer Provided:

You ask a simple question that likely requires a complicated answer. As well, since we don't know what professional field you are seeking work in, we need to make some assumptions.

You are asking about a CV. This would presume that you are a professional of some sort.

Have you considered recreating your CV into a resume format?

CVs, traditionally are long-winded way of telling somebody everything that you have done throughout your life. They are focused on what you have done i.e. in the past.

The employer is only interested in what you can do for them... now. They have a problem to solve.

A well-written resume, leading with a powerful positioning statement, can grab the employer's attention with the possibility you might be their solution.

The Experience section of your resume should be crafted to highlight the skills you developed while performing at a specific job. The idea is that the employer sees what you have done and considers the possibility that you can do the same for them.

Keep the CV up to date though as some employers still ask for them.

As for 'boosting' your CV... in addition to going the resume route, at the risk of stating the obvious, apply for jobs you are qualified for. Look for 'buzz' words in the job listing and factor them into your resume. Every job application should have a unique resume. A one-size-fits-all resume doesn't work anymore.

Maximize your Linkedin profile for effectiveness. Your Linkedin profile should resonate with your resume. The value here is that you can expand upon items you have added to your resume. Where your resume needs to be laser-focused, your Linkedin profile can expand upon your accomplishments.

As answered on Quora.com.

$\sim$

37. QUESTION: IF YOU WISH TO HAVE A SKILL IN AN AREA, IS IT RIGHT TO ADD THE SKILL TO YOUR CV WHEN YOU HAVE YET TO ACQUIRE IT?

Answer Provided:

No, definitely not!

A CV by nature, is a synopsis of the journey through your professional career. That doesn't include fantasy trips into the future.

There is nothing wrong with identifying skills you would like to have and taking actions towards achieving them. They would be better used within a job interview where you are asked how you are working on improving yourself.

If you were to make mention of it as identified in your question, it may take any credibility away from you in an interviewer's mind and you really don't to have that working against you.

So short version... no, don't do it.

As answered on Quora.com.

38. QUESTION: SHOULD I CHANGE MY RESUME ACCORDING TO THE REQUIREMENTS OF A JOB POSITION?

Answer Provided:

Only if you want to get invited in for an interview.

The days of only having one, static resume are long gone.

Your resume should resonate with the requirements of the job you are applying. You should look for key words or 'buzz' words in the job posting and factor them into your resume.

Yes, it does mean having multiple versions of your resume if it takes you a while to land a job.

While your resume should be laser-focused on the target job, it should also resonate with your Linkedin profile. Where you need to be terse and succinct on your resume, you can expand upon individual items in your Linkedin profile.

If a cover letter is requested, you should also customize it. The more of them you create, the easier it gets. If you keep electronic copies, you can easily cut and paste and with a little editing you can have a unique letter.

As answered on Quora.com.

39. QUESTION: HOW DO I WRITE MY RESUME TO HIGHLIGHT MY PAST AND ACADEMIC EXPERIENCE IN HEALTH POLICY INSTEAD OF MY CURRENT ADMIN EXPERIENCE?

Answer Provided:

If you haven't already, I would encourage you to change how you think about resumes.

Don't think of it as being a static, single version resume.

Your resume should be customized for the specific job you are targeting. In time, it will mean that you will have multiple versions of your resume.

If you are wanting to focus on your past academic experience in health policy you will need to do some brain storming and identify all the different tasks, challenges and skills that you developed during that time.

You don't provide whether all your experience was while in school i.e. academia, or if you actually have some job experience to draw upon.

Were there any problems you helped solve? Did you work on any kind of a task force? Was it successful?

Taking a close look at a specific job posting, are there any keywords or buzz words that pop out?

If so, and I expect there would be, you should factor them into your resume. Robot applicant tracking systems filter resumes by keywords. You want your resume passed on to a human rather than the trash bin.

Rather than opening with an Objective Statement, start off with a strong Positioning Statement that encapsulates who you are and what you have to offer.

You don't define what your current admin experience entails, but you should be able to leverage it to highlight why you are even better now with health policy matters.

As answered on Quora.com.

～

40. QUESTION: HOW SHOULD I LIST AN EMPLOYMENT GAP OF 7 YEARS ON MY CV?

Answer Provided:

As has been suggested, you shouldn't draw attention to the fact you haven't been in the workforce for 7 years.

However, you definitely need to be prepared to answer a question about it, should you get to a job interview.

At the very least, the interviewer may be curious. At the most, they are doing their due diligence.

While there are numerous reasons that a person may be out of the workforce for that length of time, all valid, it does raise one's curiosity. Many would wonder if there has been a lengthy prison term involved.

It also depends on if this is the first job you are seeking after the gap or if you have had other jobs since then. If you have had other jobs since the gap, it is likely moot.

If you are coming off the seven-year gap, you will likely need to mitigate the effect it has on your employability.

When you were off, did you do any training or any activities that would add to your skills or experience?

Not knowing what field or profession you were working in before you were off, I'm left wondering if your former work experience and skills are relevant? You may need to be prepared to have to defend and promote the value of your previous work experience, if it is relevant to a job you are applying for.

As answered on Quora.com.

~

41. QUESTION: WHAT DOES THE SUPERVISOR MEAN BY THIS 'INTERESTED APPLICANTS ARE ENCOURAGED TO SEND THEIR APPLICATION DOCUMENTS (COVER LETTER, CV, CERTIFICATES, DESCRIPTION OF RESEARCH EXPERIENCE, AND MOTIVATION) AS ONE PDF DOCUMENT PER E-MAIL'?

Answer Provided:

It would mean starting off with a blank Word or alternative word processing document and importing all the requested elements into it.

I would create individual documents for your cover letter, CV, description of research experience and your motivation for applying for the job. Developing them separately allows you to focus on each segment.

As for certificates, you will likely need to scan them to make them digital. Then you will need to save it as a jpg.

Back to your original document, start with your cover letter, then insert your CV etc. Then insert the jpgs of your certificates.

Save this amalgamated file as a pdf. I would suggest saving with a recognizable name e.g. your_name_job-title_application_today's date.pdf.

As answered on Quora.com.

42. QUESTION: WHAT SHOULD A JOB SEEKER ON LINKEDIN INCLUDE IN THEIR PROFILE?

Answer Provided:

Once upon a time, your Linkedin profile could be like your resume on steroids. Those days are gone.

Your resume should be crafted and fine-tuned to meet the requirements of a specific job you are applying for. Where your resume is better off being short and sweet, your Linkedin profile, which should resonate with your resume, can be a little longer.

Linkedin allows you to expand upon the job experience you have gained. It also allows you to showcase your transferrable skills you wouldn't have room to feature in your resume.

One of the common mistakes I see that job seekers make is they don't identify in the beginning of their profile they are looking for work or seeking a position.

When you are job seeking, your Linkedin profile needs to be self-promotional in nature. The employer is checking out your profile because they are interested in you, to rule you in or rule you out. They may even be checking you out before you apply for a job.

Your Linkedin profile needs to set you up as a solution to the employer's problem.

Your Linkedin profile can be a good place to add personal testimonials about you. This is different than your references.

As answered on Quora.com.

~

43. QUESTION: IF YOU'RE A JOB SEEKER WITH BEAUTIFUL PENMANSHIP, SHOULD YOU CONSIDER HAND-WRITING YOUR COVER LETTERS AS A WAY TO STAND OUT?

Answer Provided:

Not unless you were applying for a job as a calligrapher.

While you want to stand out as being different from the other applicants, you don't want to stand out in a bad way.

Handwritten business correspondence is old-fashioned nowadays. The reader may very well find it to be annoying. Many people have gotten away from reading handwriting and their minds have gotten lazy.

Cursive writing may very well become a secret code in the future, as many primary schools have dropped it in favour of keyboarding.

The only handwritten notes I can recall receiving in many years, is an annual birthday card from my sister, where she wishes me well and shares her latest updates.

While standing out is good, you would have better success in applying for jobs you are qualified for, have a strong background in the type of work and be prepared to interview well.

You can still wow them in your cover-letter, just do it with your content, rather than your handwriting.

Good luck in your job search.

As answered on Quora.com.

❧

44. QUESTION: WHAT DO YOU THINK OF PEOPLE WHO PUT THEIR IQ ON THEIR RESUME?

Answer Provided:

While there is no hard and fast rule says you can't do it, I would have to question the reason for adding it in the first place?

I can guess they feel having a high IQ posted on their resume, would give them some sort of an advantage in the job they are applying for.

However, I'm wondering from the Interviewer's perspective, if it makes them look desperate and perhaps vane?

I don't have any hard evidence to back it up either way, only opinion. I certainly wouldn't do it. But then again, I'm not a member of MENSA.

As answered on Quora.com.

～

45. QUESTION: SHOULD I LIST MY RESPONSIBILITIES ON MY RESUME?

Answer Provided:

Yes, you should list your responsibilities. No, you should not list your responsibilities on your resume.

It is a good practice to look at all of the responsibilities you have in any job. I would suggest making a master list to keep track of them all.

When it comes to creating a resume, it should be crafted to meet the requirements of a specific job posting. From your master list, see if there are any responsibilities that connect to what they are looking for in the position. If you have some and presumably you would if you were applying for the job in the first place, then list them on your resume.

If you haven't already, create a Linkedin professional profile. Under the Experience section, you can list your current responsibilities in greater detail. Any potential employer will check out your Linkedin profile as part of their hiring process. If you have more, appropriate information listed there, it can likely give you some advantage.

You may need to give some thought to how you feature your responsibilities/duties. You need to quantify and qualify them.

Examples: Why are they important? Did you work independently? Did somebody closely oversee your work or were you fairly independent? Did you use any leadership skills in your current position? Are the skills you currently use in your position transferable to the new job?

As answered on Quora.com.

~

46. QUESTION: HOW DO I ADD A PART TIME TEACHING ENGAGEMENT TO MY RESUME?

Answer Provided:

I believe it fits under the **Experience Section** of your resume.

In a resume, *experience*, is another way for saying employers are looking for positions you have held in the past.

Here is an excerpt on the topic from my book **'You're Hired! Job Search Strategies That Work'**:

The *'Old School'* way of completing this section would be to list all your skills to showcase how experienced you were under each job listing.

Here is yet another example of how times have changed.

The purpose of this section is to highlight your top three to five qualifications to a potential employer, from each previous job position.

Your content needs to be crafted so it features you as a solution to the Employer's problem.

If you include this section and you should... use a bullet format and highlight only the skills and/or qualifications are relevant to the position you are applying for.

And substantiate with a *brief* explanation of the experience(s) that helped you build the skill or quality.

Career experts recommend you customize your resumé for *each* job, especially at the beginning of your resumé.

General or generic resumes *do not work* in today's labour market.

Employers value the skills you have developed, regardless of where you developed them.

This includes skills developed in school, volunteering, extra-curricular activities and in paid employment. Since many employers use past performances to determine whether a candidate will be successful on the job or not; emphasize what you can offer potential employers (or bring to the table) drawing upon your collective experiences, skills, accomplishments, training/education and capabilities.

Validate all relevant successes and contributions made to past employers using numbers, dollars or percentages wherever possible.

Link your experience, skills and abilities to the competency requirements of the job you are applying for using examples of past successes on the job; this will enable the recruiter or hiring manager to visualize you performing the same or a similar role successfully for their organization.

Whatever you add to your resume, should resonate with what you have posted in your Linkedin profile.

As answered on Quora.com.

≈

47. QUESTION: SINCE PERSONAL BRAND IS EVERYTHING THESE DAYS, SHOULD I PUT A PROFESSIONAL SELFIE ON MY RESUME?

Answer Provided:

While I believe personal branding is a good idea for any professional, whether they have celebrity status or not, I wouldn't go as far as to say it is everything these days.

I wouldn't add a photo to a resume. I would recommend you do though, on your Linkedin profile. Odds are if the employer is interested in you, they are going to check out your Linkedin profile to see what you look like.

Forget the selfie idea. Selfies are for Facebook and Instagram. Looking for work is serious business and your head-shot photo should look professional. You can easily get somebody else to take the photo for you without the selfie's outstretched arm phenomena.

As answered on Quora.com.

~

48. QUESTION: I SENT MY RESUME AND RECOMMENDATION TO A COMPANY FOR AN INTERNSHIP. THE SECRETARY INVITED ME TO CONNECT WITH HER ON LINKEDIN AFTER ABOUT THREE WEEKS. IS THIS A POSITIVE SIGN?

A nswer Provided:

This isn't necessarily a sign of anything at all. It could merely be a coincidence.

Linkedin sends invitations from seemingly random people. Perhaps you checked out the company's Linkedin profile at one point in time.

I don't know if Linkedin does it or not, but they may have an algorhythm that matches you with employees or those connected to the company. And then sends you an invite.

If there was a message that came with the invitation from the secretary, you could further develop the relationship. As well, if there wasn't, you can still nurture the relationship.

Send them a message, mentioning you were interested in working there and had suggested an internship and having applied, but not put any pressure on them to help you get the job.

Developing internal connections can be an effective way to gain a job.

As answered on Quora.com.

49. QUESTION: SHOULD YOU INCLUDE YOUR LINKEDIN PUBLIC PROFILE URL ON YOUR RESUME?

Answer Provided:

No, you should not include your Linkedin *profile* on your resume. However, you should insert your Linkedin Public Profile URL.

This should be placed at the bottom of and part of your Contact Information.

The interviewer is likely to research you on-line anyways. This saves them a step.

Your resume should resonate with your Linkedin profile. Whereas your resume should be tailored for a specific job opportunity, your Linkedin profile allows you to expand upon your skills & experience.

Your Linkedin profile can also be a good place to add testimonials. These are in addition to any references you have lined up to speak favorably about you.

Make sure you have optimized your Linkedin profile for effectiveness.

As answered on Quora.com.

50. QUESTION: HOW SOON MAY I PUT A POSITION ON MY RESUME? I JUST STARTED A PART-TIME POSITION (TWO WEEKS AGO) THAT WILL CONTINUE, AS I APPLY FOR SUMMER INTERNSHIPS. I HAVE ONLY DONE ONE PROJECT THUS FAR. IS IT TOO SOON TO PUT THE PART-TIME JOB ON MY RESUME?

A nswer Provided:

There is no rule that says when and when you can't add a job position to your resume. Or you identify and post every job you have ever had in your resume.

As you say that you are looking for summer internships, I'm going to assume that you are fairly new to the job searching process. Everyone has to start somewhere.

Something to consider is that you should look at your resume as never being 'done.' It should be a dynamic process, where you add or remove content as you go through life.

I would add your current job to your resume and then as you get a better understanding of what the job entails, add the skills you have developed in this role, to the content of this particular job.

If you haven't already, I would suggest creating a Linkedin profile and have it resonate with your resume. The two work together and your Linkedin profile can allow you to expand upon items in your resume.

As answered on Quora.com.

~

51. QUESTION: IS IT UNPROFESSIONAL TO ADD A SHORT QUOTE ON MY RESUME IN THE INTRO DESCRIPTION/COVER LETTER?

Answer Provided:

I'm not sure about it being *un*professional, but I don't think it is professional.

Your cover letter needs to be tactfully written to grab the recipient's attention.

While on one hand, you want to promote yourself in a positive way and pique your reader's interest, you don't want them to get distracted on the purpose of your letter.

You either appreciate inspirational quotes or you don't. If the reader isn't a fan, you risk alienating them. If they are a fan, there is still a risk. There focus may go towards trying to figure out the quote and what the relevance is.

If you do have an inspirational quote that resonates with you, I believe you would get better leverage out of it by inserting it into the opening promotion in your Linkedin profile.

As a potential employer/hiring manager is likely to check you out on Linkedin, it may lead to future conversation if you make it to the interview stage.

52. QUESTION: IS IT WISE TO ADD A LINKEDIN HYPERLINK IN A COVER LETTER OR RESUME?

Answer Provided:

I'm not sure if it would be considered wise or not, but it certainly could be strategic.

Odds are high the employer will check you out on Linkedin anyways.

By having your Linkedin contact info featured on your resume or cover letter with your other contact info, it saves the employer from having to Google you.

In the comment section you mention "...for a more comprehensive list of qualifications, please see my LinkedIn." This is ineffective in my opinion, as it makes your resume redundant.

Each resume you submit should be crafted for the job you are applying. If you are using your Linkedin profile as an adjunct to your resume, it needs to be consistent with the content in your resume.

While the expectation that a resume be one to two pages in length, you have a lot more freedom with your Linkedin profile. This allows you to post more comprehensive experience, that may help you in landing a job within a different field than that of what you have been working in.

Something to remember is the copy in both your resume and your Linkedin profile has to be crafted from the perspective of how you can solve the problem a perspective employer has rather than how wonderful you are and what you have done in the past.

This is a major difference from how resumes and Linkedin profiles used to be written in the not so distant past.

As answered on Quora.com.

~

53. QUESTION: SHOULD I MENTION MY GOLD MEDAL FOR BEST ACADEMIC PERFORMANCE AT UNIVERSITY ON MY RESUME, OR WILL IT LOOK BOASTFUL AND IRRELEVANT, AS IT'S BEEN 5 YEARS SINCE I GRADUATED?

Walt Whitman, American Cowboy Poet is often quoted as saying, "if you done it, it ain't bragging!"

As to its relevance, it depends on the requirements of the particular job you are applying for. Your resume should be crafted for individual jobs, not be a one-size-fits-all version.

While others might advise that including your gold medal as a waste of space as nobody will ever read it, well that's just an opinion, as is this...

If it is relevant to the duties of the position you are applying for, including it may just be the leverage point to set you a little higher than another applicant whose academic achievement isn't as stellar.

At best, it might open up a question from a curious interviewer, at worst, they will ignore it.

I think it is worth the gamble.

As answered on Quora.com.

~

54. QUESTION: IS IT PROPER TO ADD MY LAST COMPANY WHERE I WORKED AND WAS FIRED TO MY RESUME?

Answer Provided:

I wouldn't bother thinking in terms of whether it is proper or not. Far better to think in terms of asking 'is there value in posting it or not?'

Despite having been fired, there were likely skills you developed and experience you gained while employed in the job.

Your resume doesn't need to be a complete list of every job you have had, like a curriculum vitae would be. However, it should be tailored to meet the requirements of the specific job you are applying for.

If your skills and experience are relevant for the job, use it. If not, leave it out.

If you leave it out though, you will need to be prepared to answer a question about the break in your working history. Same thing applies to adding it to your resume and then being prepared for a possible question of "so why did you leave that job?"

You will likely find that as you go through life, you may very well be fired a few times. As time passes, it lessens in importance. One caveat though ... hopefully you have learned from the event.

55. QUESTION: WHAT SOUNDS BEST IN MY CV: TEACHING ASSISTANT, RESEARCH ASSISTANT, OR PERSONAL ASSISTANT OF THE PROFESSOR?

Answer Provided:

To me, they sound like three different positions as well as different duties.

What is important is you link the one you choose to the requirements of the specific job you are applying for.

You can then expand upon the duties and skills developed under the title you choose to highlight your experience.

When it comes to resume/CV writing, think of self-promotion. You want to be seen as the solution to the employer's problem.

As answered on Quora.com.

~

56. QUESTION: IN APPLYING TO DIRECTOR-LEVEL "MBA" TYPE JOBS, HOW MUCH TIME SHOULD IT BE TAKING ME TO CUSTOMIZE MY RESUME BULLETS AND COVER LETTER?

Answer Provided:

It'll take as much time as it takes to do so...

In creating a resume, if you haven't already, there is value in brainstorming a list of duties and responsibilities you have had with each of your positions. This would go into your resume data file.

When you are customizing your resume, you need to take these generated duties & responsibilities and rework the wording on them tying them into the requirements of the job requirements.

That would likely mean your resume would be substantially different for each position you apply for.

Your resume should be a dynamic tool i.e. it is always being changed to meet the requirements of a specific job.

As for the cover letter, there are likely elements such as the opening and the closing that can be reused for different applications, but the so-called meat and potatoes i.e. the body of the letter should be customized for each position.

As answered on Quora.com.

ABOUT THE AUTHOR

Rae A. Stonehouse is a Canadian born author & speaker.

His professional career as a Registered Nurse working predominantly in psychiatry/mental health, has spanned four decades.

Rae has embraced the principal of CANI (Constant and Never-ending Improvement) as promoted by thought leaders such as Tony Robbins and brings that philosophy to each of his publications and presentations.

Rae has dedicated the latter segment of his journey through life to overcoming his personal inhibitions. As a 25+ year member of Toast-masters International he has systematically built his self-confidence and communicating ability. He is passionate about sharing his lessons with his readers and listeners.

His publications thus far are of the self-help, self-improvement genre and systematically offer valuable sage advice on a specific topic.

His writing style can be described as being conversational. As an author, Rae strives to have a one-to-one conversation with each of his readers, very much like having your own personal self-development coach.

Rae is known for having a wry sense of humour that features in his publications. To learn more about Rae A. Stonehouse, visit the Wonderful World of Rae Stonehouse at http://raestonehouse.com.

facebook.com/rae.stonehouse

twitter.com/raestonehouse

PUBLICATIONS BY THE AUTHOR

Power Networking for Shy People: Tips & Techniques for Moving from Shy to Sly!

http://powernetworkingforshypeople.com

∾

PROtect Yourself! Empowering Tips & Techniques for Personal Safety: A Practical Violence Prevention Manual for Healthcare Workers
http://protectyourselfnow.ca/

∾

E=Emcee Squared: Tips & Techniques to Becoming a Dynamic Master of Ceremonies

http://emceesquared.mremcee.com/

∾

Power of Promotion: On-line Marketing for Toastmasters Club Growth

http://powerofpromotion.ca/

∾

You're Hired! Job Search Strategies That Work (This is the complete program)

E-book & Paperback: Available @ https://books2read.com/yourehired

On-line E-course: (Available as a self-directed or instructor-led program)

You're Hired! Resume Tactics: Job Search Strategies That Work

E-book & Paperback: Available @ : https://books2read.com/resumetactics

On-line E-course: http://liveforexcellenceacademy.com/

Job Interview Preparation: Job Search Strategies That Work

E-book & Paperback: Available @ books2read.com/jobinterviewpreparation

On-line E-course: http://liveforexcellenceacademy.com/

You're Hired! Leveraging Your Network: Job Search Strategies That Work

E-book & Paperback: Available @ http://books2read.com/leveragingyournetwork

On-line E-course: http://liveforexcellenceacademy.com/

You're Hired! Power Tactics: Job Search Strategies That Work (This is a box set containing the complete content of Resume Tactics, Job Interview Preparation & Leveraging Your Network)

E-book Available @ http://books2read.com/powertactics

∾

If you have found this book and program to be helpful, please leave us a warm review wherever you purchased this book.

www.ingramcontent.com/pod-product-compliance
Lightning Source LLC
Chambersburg PA
CBHW071704210326
41597CB00017B/2320